The New Instrumentation

Series Editor: Bertram Turetzky

1. *The Contemporary Contrabass*, by Bertram Turetzky, 1989. *Out of print.*
2. *The Avant-Garde Flute: A Handbook for Composers and Flutists*, by Thomas Howell, 1974. *Out of print.*
3. *The Modern Trombone: A Definition of Its Idiom*, by Stuart Dempster, 1979. *Out of print.*
4. *New Directions for Clarinet*, Revised Edition, by Phillip Rehfeldt, 2003.
5. *The Contemporary Guitar*, by John Schneider, 1985. *Out of print.*
6. *Writing for the Pedal Harp: A Standardized Manual for Composers and Harpist*, by Ruth K. Ingelfield and Lou Anne Neill, 1992. *Out of print.*
7. *The Contemporary Violin: Extended Performance Techniques*, by Patricia and Allen Strange, 2001.
8. *Oboe Unbound: Contemporary Techniques*, by Libby Van Cleve, 2004.
9. *The 21st-Century Voice*, by Michael Edgerton, 2004.

Oboe Unbound

Contemporary Techniques

Libby Van Cleve

The New Instrumentation Series, No. 8

The Scarecrow Press, Inc.
Lanham, Maryland • Toronto • Oxford
2004

SCARECROW PRESS, INC.

Published in the United States of America
by Scarecrow Press, Inc.
A wholly owned subsidiary of
The Rowman & Littlefield Publishing Group, Inc.
4501 Forbes Boulevard, Suite 200, Lanham, Maryland 20706
www.scarecrowpress.com

PO Box 317
Oxford
OX2 9RU, UK

British Library Cataloguing in Publication Information Available

Library of Congress Cataloging-in-Publication Data

Van Cleve, Libby.
  Oboe unbound : contemporary techniques / Libby Van Cleve.
    p.   cm.— (New instrumentation ; v. 8)
  Includes bibliographical references and index.
  ISBN 0-8108-5031-1 (pbk. : alk. paper)
  1. Oboe—Instruction and study.   I. Title.   II. Series.
MT360.V35 2004
788.5′2193—dc22   2004004161

♾ ™ The paper used in this publication meets the minimum requirements of American National Standard
for Information Sciences—Permanence of Paper for Printed Library Materials, ANSI/NISO Z39.48-1992.
Manufactured in the United States of America.

*To Nola—who gave me
the only deadline I had to respect,
and much much more.*

Contents

Acknowledgments

In writing this book, I received a tremendous amount of help and advice from many individuals. I would particularly like to thank the following people:

Jacqueline Leclair, Judi Scramlin, and Electra Reed O'Mara for their extraordinary generosity and dedication, spending countless hours testing fingerings and reading the text.

Nobuo Kitagawa, Jenny Raymond, and Matt Sullivan for additional help in testing fingerings and reading the text.

Ingram Marshall, Stefan Weisman, and Ruth Van Cleve for their careful reading and commentary on the text. David Heetderks and Jack Vees for help with manuscript preparation.

The many oboists who have assisted me, including Joseph Celli, Paul Laubin, James Ostryniec, Nora Post, and Harry Sargous.

The countless oboists and composers who have shared ideas and information.

Colin Cantwell for the inspiring cover art, Tom Johnson for permission to reproduce his witty and charming drawings, and Antonietta Kies for the fanciful yet accurate oboe diagram.

Arthur Jarvinen, for generous assistance with music copying and inspiration for the title of this book.

David Rosenboom for sharing the live recording of his composition, *And Come Up Dripping*, and for his diligent audio enhancement of the electronics.

The composers and publishers who have generously permitted the reproduction of their scores, including Leisure Planet Music for Jack Vees's *Apocrypha*, copyright 1986; Rugginienti Edditore, for Drake Mabry's *Lament for Astralabe*, copyright 1994; G. Schirmer, Inc., for John Corigliano's *Oboe Concerto*, copyright 1978; and James Tenney, for *Critical Band*, copyright 1998.

The librarians at the Yale University Music Library, especially Suzanne Eggleston Lovejoy, for extraordinary assistance, perseverance, and kindness.

Vivian Perlis, for her patience and flexibility, her suggestions regarding writing style, and the constant inspiration she is for those who know her.

The staff at Scarecrow Press, particularly Kellie Hagan, Bruce Phillips, and Sam Grammer, for their expertise and support.

The Music Department at Wesleyan University and the Vice President's Office of Fairfield University for financial support.

The musicians and authors who have come before me and whose work I have drawn upon, including Heinz Holliger, Lawrence Singer, Nora Post, Robert Dick, Phillip Rehfeldt, Bertram Turetzky, Peter Veale, Andrea Chenna, and Massimiliano Salmi.

My beloved teachers, Basil Reeve, Ronald Roseman, and Allan Vogel.

Jack Vees, who assisted me with the text and computer graphics, who survived countless squawking practice sessions and nerdy dinner table discussions about esoteric oboe issues, who knew just when to nag and be impatient with my procrastination, and whose humor, love, and support have helped everything.

CHAPTER ONE

Introduction

Decades have passed since Bartolozzi's groundbreaking book, *New Sounds for Woodwind*, and the first wave of experimentation and development that followed. Excellent books, such as Phillip Rehfeldt's *New Directions for Clarinet* and Robert Dick's *The Other Flute*, became invaluable manuals for performers as well as composers. As a student, I was intensely curious about extended techniques and frustrated by the lack of resources available for the oboe. I foraged for bits of information, learned what my teachers could offer, and spent a lot of time working with composers and developing my own repertoire of sounds. In writing this book, my goal has been to present practical and reliable information for oboists and composers interested in these contemporary techniques. It is meant as a point of departure, to stimulate musicians to explore more fully the instrument's sonic potential.

It was only when I began to share information that I understood the problems inherent in

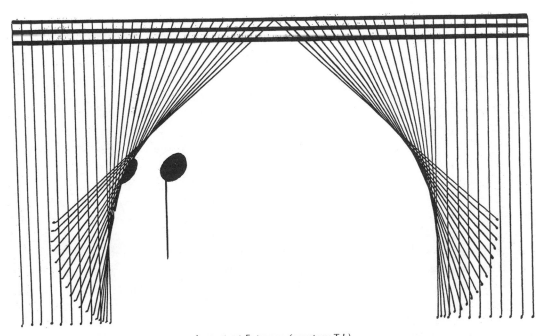

Important Entrance (courtesy T.J.)

standardizing technical information for the oboe. Differences in reed types, bore types, and makes and models of oboes all present challenges. To address these, I asked musicians who play different types of oboes with differing reed styles to test all the fingerings in this book. The oboists who have tested the fingerings are Jacqueline Leclair, Nobuo Kitagawa, Jenny Raymond, Judi Scramlin, Electra Reed O'Mara, and Matthew Sullivan. Fingerings were tested on oboes made by Laubin, Lorée, Marigaux, Rigoutat, and Buffet; on oboes made of rosewood and grenadilla wood; and on oboes with a variety of reeds typically played in the United States. All of the testers play on a variation of the American long scrape reed that is generally described in *The Oboe Reed Book* by Jay Light.[1]

Readers can refer to the chart at the end of the book for a diagram of oboe keys and an explanation of symbols used to indicate embouchure pressures, lip pressures, and reed positions. When working with these techniques, composers should hear and test out any unfamiliar sounds with sympathetic oboe players rather than simply follow this book.

Standard Oboe Technique

Range and Dynamics

The lowest note on the oboe is the B flat below middle C, Bb_3.[2] Some players have experimented and added a device that extends the bottom range, but this is not standardized, and composers should not expect most players to perform any pitch lower than the Bb. It is difficult for many oboists to play quietly in the extreme low range. A full range of dynamics can be easily achieved from approximately the low Eb (Eb_4) to the high C (C_6). The highest note that the oboe can play has been extended over time. Mozart's magnificent Oboe Quartet, KV370, goes up to a high F (F_6). Any professional oboist should be able to reach this note with confidence and good intonation. Many contemporary pieces reach to G_6 or A_6. Berio's *Sequenza VII* goes up to the G. The A is the highest pitch in pieces that range from such classics as Krenek's *Four Pieces for Oboe and Piano* and Wolpe's *Suite im Hexachord* to more recent notable compositions, such as Ligeti's *Double Concerto* and concerti by Elliott Carter and John Corigliano. Most oboists can play these notes competently. As the pitch rises, the note becomes more unstable and difficult to play in tune. Extremely high notes tend to be thin in tone and somewhat quiet. See chapter 2 for more discussion on the upper register and a list of fingerings.

Oboists need to adjust their embouchure throughout the instrument's register. In general, low notes are produced with a fairly open embouchure and very little reed in the mouth. As oboists approach the upper register, they usually use somewhat more lip pressure and put a little more reed into the mouth. Slurring between extremes of register can be done very smoothly, but this requires substantial flexibility of the embouchure. It's usually easier to slur from low to high than from high to low. Extreme high notes often require awkward fingerings, and composers should keep this in mind when writing speedy passages in this register.

The dynamic range of the oboe is somewhat more limited than it is for other wind instruments. For example, clarinetists can more easily produce whisper-quiet notes and perfect diminuendos into silence, and saxophonists can more easily play a true fortissimo. Nevertheless, a professional oboist should be able to produce quiet attacks and diminuendos throughout the range of the instrument as well as create substantial volume.

Figure 1-1   Oboe range

English Horn and Oboe d'Amore

This book focuses primarily on oboe technique; however, applications for the English horn and oboe d'amore will be included throughout. (See figure 1-2.) The English horn is in the

English Horn:

written   sounding

Oboe D'amore:

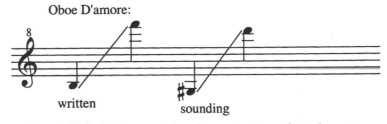

written   sounding

Figure 1-2   English horn and oboe d'amore written and sounding range

key of F, and its lowest note is the written B_3 (sounding E_3). Some English horns can produce the written B flat below middle C, and one can buy an extension to produce this note, but this is not the standard setup. Composers should not expect the instrument to play below the written B. The highest note has also been extended over time. It is harder to play the English horn in the extreme high range (written F_6 and beyond), and there is little use of this register in traditional literature. The oboe d'amore is in the key of A, and its lowest note is the written B_3 (sounding $G\sharp_3$). Indications for the high range are similar to those for the English horn. Both instruments use reeds that are slightly larger than oboe reeds. These reeds are put on a bocal, a metal tube with cork on the end that is inserted into the top joint of the instrument.

Breathing

One of the unique aspects of oboe technique is the very small amount of breath it takes to play the instrument. If you look at the tiny opening of an oboe reed, you can see that only a small volume of air could possibly go through it. This is one of the reasons that oboists can play very long phrases (and can stay under water longer than most human beings). Unlike most other wind players, oboists will often exhale as well as inhale with every breath on the instrument. It is not uncommon, especially in long passages such as those frequently found in Baroque music, for players to exhale, play a phrase, and then inhale. The oboe requires a small volume of air, but a great deal of air pressure. (This accounts for contorted red faces and the prevalent belief that playing the oboe will drive you mad. Of course, many oboists are pretty close to the edge, but we know that it is due to making our own reeds and the emotional extremes necessary for playing Bach arias and Mahler!) Composers must consider the breath when writing for oboists. The music will sound better if the oboist has a good chance to breathe. This may seem obvious, but many composers write music that overly taxes the oboist—and both the music and the musician suffer for it. See chapter 4 for information on circular breathing.

Tuning and Intonation
Wind players love to quip, "I know I'm in tune—my horn was tuned at the factory!" If only it were that easy. Oboes, even the highest quality ones made from the best manufacturers, are acoustical systems with compromised tuning. Players need to listen carefully and adjust pitches accordingly. Most instruments tend to be a bit flat in the lower register and sharp in the extreme upper register. Certain notes will be predictably out of tune. For example, almost every oboe is sharp on E_5, $F\#_5$, and G_5, and many oboes are stuffy and flat on $C\#_4$. The temperature of the room will affect intonation: heat will make the pitch rise, while cold will make it lower. Oboists can easily adjust the intonation of a note by changing the reed position or lip pressure: putting a little more reed in the mouth or tightening the embouchure will raise the pitch, and pulling the reed out or loosening the embouchure will lower it.

Articulation
In standard oboe technique, the tip of the reed extends into the mouth, just past the teeth, and the tongue rests at the base of the mouth. To prepare a note, the tip of the tongue moves to the tip of the lower blade of the reed, and air pressure, embouchure, and support are in place. When the tongue leaves the reed, the tone begins. (This phenomenon might be better referred to as the "release" of a note rather than "attack.") Players imagine pronouncing the syllable "tee." Breath attacks are softer and are achieved by starting the note without using the tongue. Accented notes are achieved by using a greater volume of air, often accompanied by faster movement of the tongue and sometimes using the diaphragm to achieve a breath accent. Notes are ended with a combination of increased embouchure and decreased air pressure. It is rare to use the tongue to end a note, unless a particularly abrupt sound is desired.

For speedy articulation, the tip of the tongue touches the lower blade of the reed but does not come to complete rest at the base of the mouth. Most oboists can comfortably tongue an average sixteenth-note passage with a metronome speed that ranges from 112 to 152, depending on the individual. Many oboists use double tonguing to achieve very fast articulation. (See chapter 4 for a discussion of double tonguing.) Fast articulation is more difficult on the lowest few notes on the instrument because there is a tendency for them to crack (i.e., sound an octave higher).

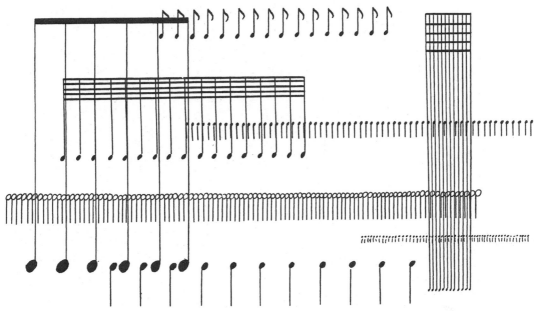

Composition with Repeated Notes (courtesy T.J.)

Reeds

The oboe is a conical acoustic system with the reed at the vertex or tip, a point of great sensitivity to the entire system. This begins to explain why the reed is of such fundamental importance to the operation of the instrument. Most oboists make their own reeds, and they can control the pitch, stability, flexibility, and sound—at least to the degree of their reed-making skills and the whims of the cane. Oboe reeds vary a great deal around the world, within regions of one country, and even between individuals in the same basic school of oboe playing.

Despite obsessive reed making, curses, and prayers, most oboists have come to accept the sad truth that a perfect reed does not exist. This is as true for the performance of an extended technique improvisation as for a Brahms symphony. After much experimentation, it is my preference to play most contemporary music on a light, flexible, responsive reed, the type I would use to perform the Mozart Oboe Quartet. The tip needs to be light, and the entire reed should be stable enough so that players don't have to use much bite in their embouchures. For extended techniques, as in any performance situation, reeds need to match the demands of the piece. Honking multiphonics come out best when played on heavy reeds with wide openings, whereas extreme high notes are played more easily with lighter reeds and narrower openings. Oboists should experiment with their own individual reed styles to determine what works best for them.

Notes

1. Jay Light, *The Oboe Reed Book* (Des Moines, Iowa: Drake University: 1983).

2. On MIDI keyboards, middle C is often referred to as C_3, whereas it has traditionally been known as C_4. Throughout the text, the traditional references will be used. Refer to the chart in the back of the book for a diagram.

CHAPTER TWO

~

Monophonic Techniques

This chapter includes directions for the performance of monophonic, or single-sounding, techniques. Harmonics, alternate timbres, microtones, glissandi and pitch bends, and upper-register fingerings will be discussed. The chart at the end of the book defines all notational and fingering symbols.

Harmonics

Oboe harmonics are produced by opening an octave key so as to overblow a low note to sound an octave and a fifth higher. For example, the harmonic shown below is fingered D_4 with the second octave key open, and this produces the pitch A_5. Harmonics can produce an ethereal and hollow sound. Played quietly and with no vibrato, passages consisting of harmonics can sound ghostly and distant.[1]

The range of harmonics on the oboe is from F_5 to C_6. Some pure harmonic fingerings are unstable and unreliable; therefore, slight adjustments are suggested that don't significantly alter the timbre. Figure 2-1 shows standard notation for harmonics: put the harmonic symbol above the note to be heard, not the note to be fingered.

One of the earliest pieces that calls for harmonics is Stefan Wolpe's *Suite im Hexachord* for oboe and clarinet, as shown in figure 2-2. Harmonics are sometimes used alternating with normal fingerings for a subtle shift in timbre as in John Corigliano's Oboe Concerto, as shown in figure 2-3.

Harmonics need not be thought of as an extended technique to be used only in rare and precious moments. I frequently use harmonics for standard repertoire when I want a different tone color or a sound that blends easily for the inner voice of a chord. Note that double harmonics are actually a type of multiphonic that will be discussed in chapter 3.

Harmonics are produced using the same principle for all members of the oboe family. Oboe d'amore and English horn harmonics have an ethereal and hollow sound quality that is similar to but somewhat richer and darker than the timbre of oboe harmonics. The keywork on the lower horns is usually slightly different from that on an oboe: the lower horns do not have a hole in the G key (called a split G key) or a low B♭ key, so fingerings using the G half hole or B♭ keys are inapplicable. In other words, no fingerings that include a half closing on the G key (the third key from the top) or with a written "B♭" in the center right would be applicable

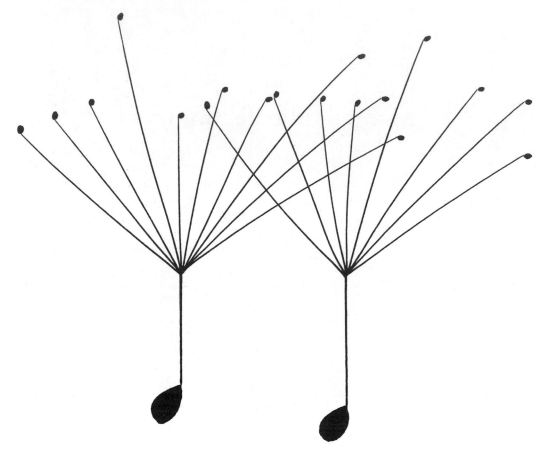

Quarter Notes with Overtones (courtesy T.J.)

Figure 2-1   Harmonics notation

pp

Figure 2-2   Wolpe, Suite im Hexachord

Figure 2-3   Corigliano, Oboe Concerto

on the English horn or oboe d'amore. Harmonics on the lower horns begin on written F♯₅, an octave and a fifth above the instrument's lowest note.

Ingram Marshall's *Dark Waters* juxtaposes the lowest and richest tones of the English horn with light, floating harmonics, as shown in figure 2-4.

Figure 2-4   Marshall, Dark Waters

Alternative Timbre Fingerings

A variety of timbres can be achieved on almost every oboe tone by using alternative fingerings. Perhaps the best-known piece that employs this technique is Berio's *Sequenza VII* in which the oboist is asked to find five different timbres for a single note (see figure 2-6). Berio suggests fingerings that range from a standard fingering with a few other keys depressed, to an overblown octave B, and finally to highly unorthodox fingerings.

Eleanor Hovda uses alternative fingerings to produce a constantly changing, churning, and moving texture in *Record of an Ocean Cliff* (see figure 2-7). This effect is mostly achieved by adding and subtracting keys to the standard fingering.[2] Jack Vees's *Apocrypha* includes alternate fingerings, harmonics, and multiphonics emerging from a single tone, all accompanied by haunting electronic sounds made by recording the resonance of the oboe in a piano (see figure 2-8). Vees includes specific suggestions for each alternate fingering and multiphonic. A score of this entire piece is included in appendix 2, and a recording is on CD track 36.

A variety of notations has been used to indicate alternative fingerings. Sometimes composers simply include a verbal indication (e.g., Hovda); sometimes they include specific suggestions for fingerings with an asterisk (e.g., Vees). Elliott Carter wrote the initials "N S N S N S" above a single pitch. "N" indicated the normal fingering, whereas "S" indicated an altered fingering. He included a footnote to explain his notation (shown in figure 2-9).

Some composers use the notation "N O N O N O" in which "N" indicates a normal fingering and "O" indicates an altered fingering. This indication is potentially confusing and misleading because a circle above a note usually indicates a harmonic. Takemitsu used this notation in *Distance* (see figure 2-10). Bartolozzi drew note heads with different shapes in his

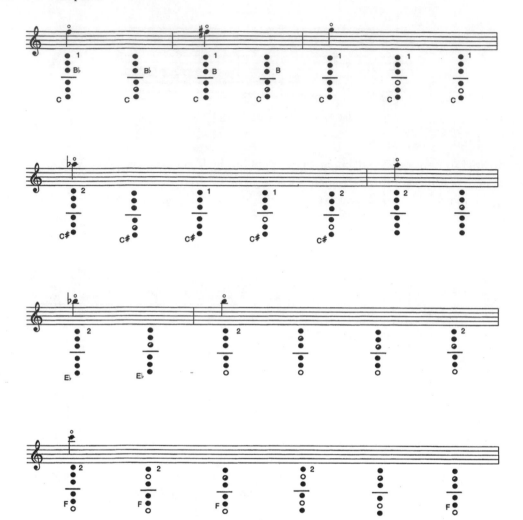

Figure 2-5   Fingering chart of harmonics

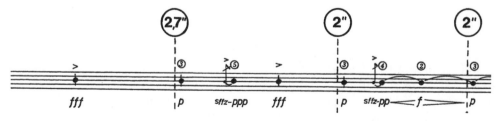

Figure 2-6   Berio, Sequenza VII

Figure 2-7   Hovda, Record of an Ocean Cliff

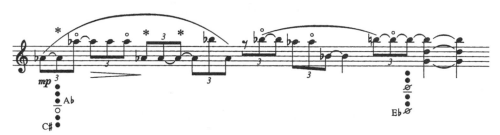

Figure 2-8   Vees, Apocrypha

Figure 2-9   Carter, Sonata for flute, oboe, cello, and harpsichord

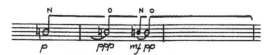

Figure 2-10   Takemitsu, Distance

Figure 2-11   Bartolozzi, Concertazioni

Concertazioni (see figure 2-11). In *Solo* for oboe, Denisov used "O + O + O +" above a pitch. "O" indicated the ordinary fingering (not a harmonic!), and "+" indicated the altered fingering. He also included an explanatory note (see figure 2-12).

Since the notation of alternate fingerings is not standardized, composers should always include an explanatory note to make sure their intentions are understood. It is helpful for the

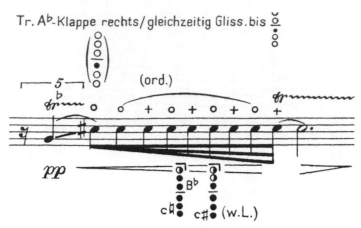

Figure 2-12 Denisov, Solo

composer to recommend possible fingerings while allowing some flexibility for the individual preferences of the performer.

Alternate timbres are easily produced on all members of the oboe family. These timbres can be especially effective on the lower instruments because of their inherent richness of tone. As stated above, the lower horns are usually constructed without a split G key or a B♭ key, so fingerings noted below that use the G half hole or B♭ key are inapplicable. However, it is often possible to substitute the B key when the B♭ key is noted, as shown in figure 2-13.

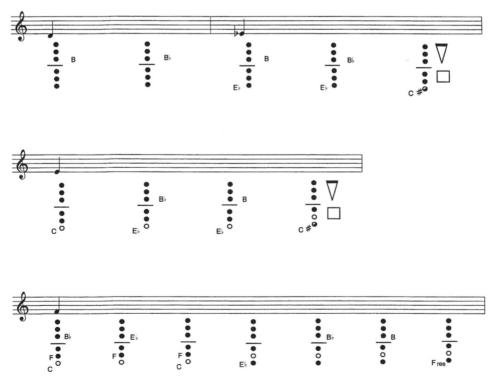

Figure 2-13   Alternative timbre fingerings

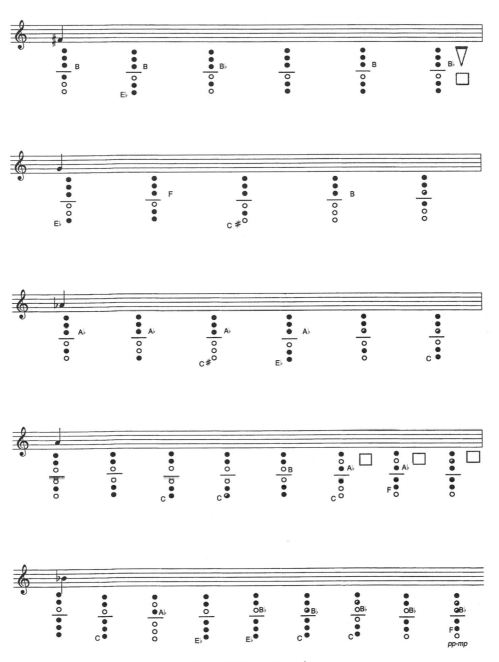

Figure 2-13   continued

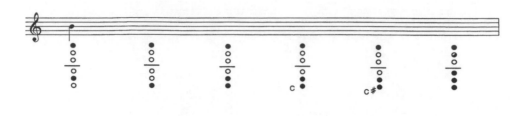

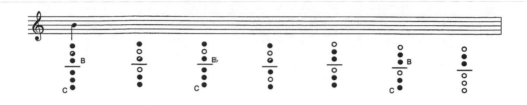

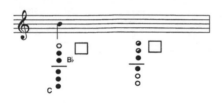

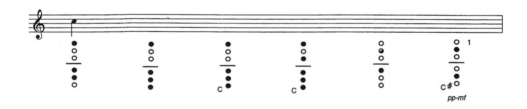

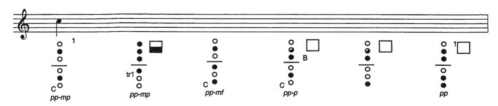

Figure 2-13   continued

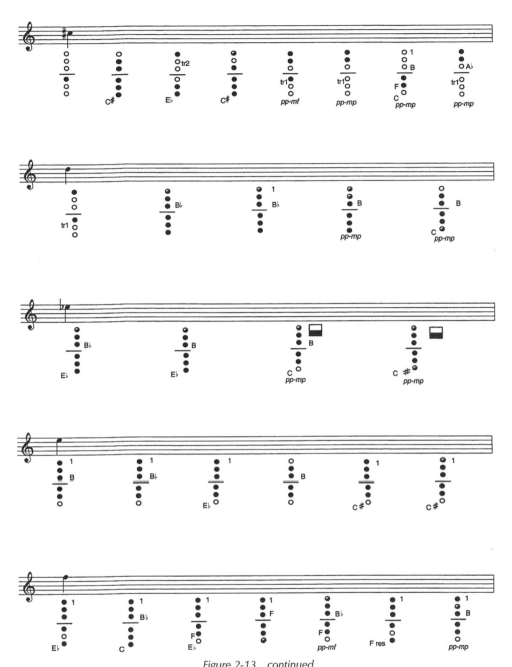

Figure 2-13   continued

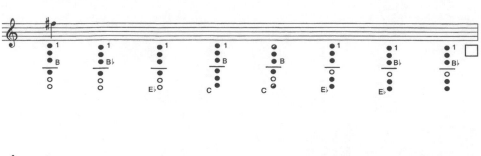

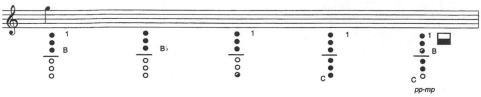

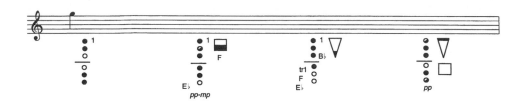

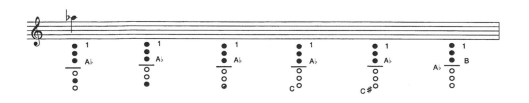

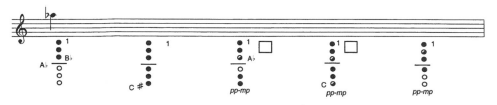

Figure 2-13   continued

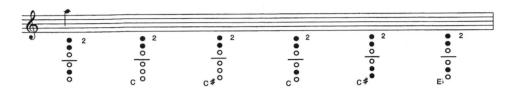

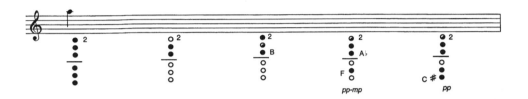

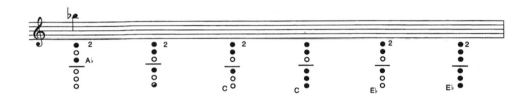

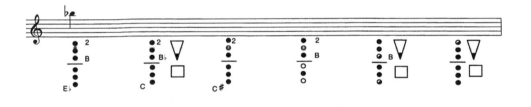

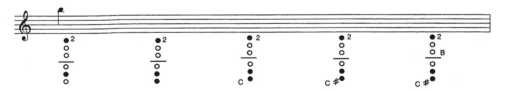

Figure 2-13 continued

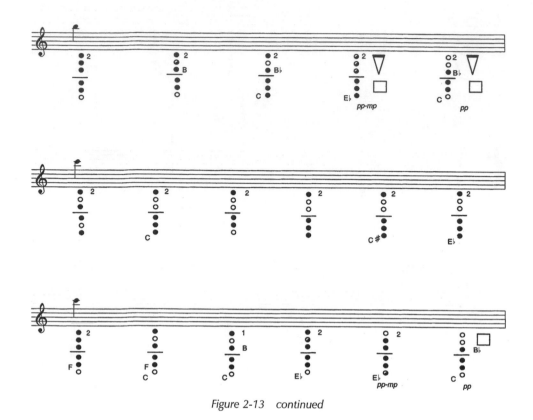

Figure 2-13   continued

Quarter Tones and Microtones

When I speak to composers, I often point out that the oboe is naturally a microtonal instrument—certain notes on the instrument always need major adjustment, and all of them are very flexible with minor embouchure changes. As noted in chapter 1, the tuning of the oboe, even for equal temperament, is imperfect and compromised. Quarter tones and smaller intervals are relatively easy to play on the oboe. The basic approach is to take the standard fingering and either slightly raise or slightly lower it with the addition or subtraction of keys. For example, if one plays the standard fingering for a "G" (all the keys of the top joint) and adds the "E" key (the middle key of the second joint), the pitch will lower. More difficult for most players is the ear training involved in playing microtonal music. Composers from Harry Partch through Ben Johnston to the youngest experimenters today have devised widely varying systems of intonation, from 43-tone scales to intervals of $1/3$ to $1/8$ to $1/12$ of a semi-tone. Each varying system requires performers to refine and newly train their hearing. Tuners and synthesizers can be used to aid in the process. The following musical examples all demand precise intonation, and the player is aided by the musical context.

In the brief gesture shown, Harvey Sollberger has accompanied the oboe with a piano on the G and a cello harmonic on a C (see figure 2-14). This juxtaposition of pitches and the

Figure 2-14   Sollberger, Three or Four Things I Know about the Oboe

oboe's playing style—*forte, pesante,* and strongly articulated—highlights the quarter tones. Drake Mabry's *Lament for Astralabe* (see figure 2-15) uses quarter tones as a type of ornament. By placing quarter tones next to adjacent tones, he achieves a hyper-chromaticism.

James Tenney's *Critical Band* requires very precise intonation from all players (see figure 2-16). Tenney indicates the specific number of cents above or below A 440. This is challenging, but there is always the sound of the fundamental A 440 to tune to. Quarter-tone fingerings given below may be adjusted with the embouchure, and additional keys may be added or removed to achieve these fingerings.

A variety of notations has been used to indicate quarter-tone and microtonal fingerings.

Figure 2-15   Mabry, Lament for Astralabe

Three approaches are shown in figure 2-17. Figure 2-18 shows a precise chart, indicating cents and relation of pitches to a fundamental pitch for Harry Partch's 43-tone scale using Ben Johnston's notation.

In reading quarter-tone music, I prefer the notation using arrows on accidentals because it is the most intuitive. This is the notation used in Shinohara's *Réflexion,* Holliger's *Studie II,* and Sollberger's *Three or Four Things I Know about the Oboe* to name only a few examples. However, if smaller intervals are desired, this system is limited.

The quarter-tone fingering chart in figure 2-19 begins with an E♭$_4$ and ends with a G♯$_6$. It is possible to play quarter tones lower or higher than those listed; however, these notes are very unstable and require substantial embouchure adjustment. The following list includes fingerings that produce approximately true quarter tones with little embouchure adjustment. Because of the wide variety of potential tuning systems, it is difficult to list all the possible fingerings to produce all the permutations of pitch that might be called for. Instead, I present here a group of stable and reliable quarter-tone fingerings that can be altered by adding or subtracting keys, by putting more or less reed in the mouth, or by tightening or loosening the embouchure.[3]

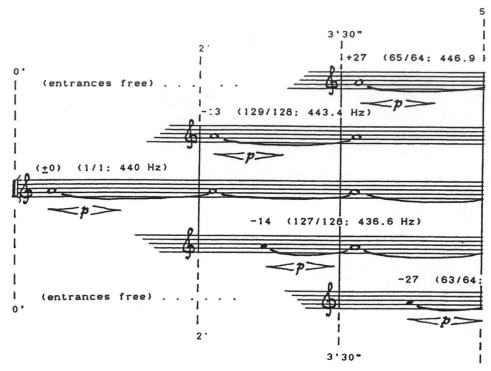

Figure 2-16 Tenney, Critical Band

Quarter tones and microtones are as easy to produce on the English horn and oboe d'amore as on the oboe. Their pitch flexibility is also limited in the extreme low and high registers. As stated above, the lower horns usually do not have a split G key or a B♭ key; therefore, fingerings using the G half hole or B♭ key are inapplicable, but the B key can sometimes be substituted for the B♭ key.

Glissandi and Pitch Bends

One of the great ecstatic experiences of all times comes in hearing the sound of Bizmallah Khan glissing over an octave on his shenai, the North Indian quadruple-reed cousin of the oboe. A reason this gliss sounds so extraordinary is that the shenai has no keys. The best oboe to produce a glissando is the open-hole or ring-model oboe, but this instrument is rarely used today because its intonation is poor. So we are left with the standard oboe in which glissandi are very difficult to achieve with consistency over an extended range. In addition, it is not possible to achieve a true gliss over the break, which is C_5 to $C\#_5$. To move between these notes, one must go from a fingering with only the two index fingers depressed to a fingering with all the fingers down. If a gliss over these notes is necessary, the player needs to alter his or her embouchure in the method described below for pitch bends when crossing the break. It is difficult to achieve this smoothly.

The most effective glissando is achieved by gradually sliding fingers off the hole, then off

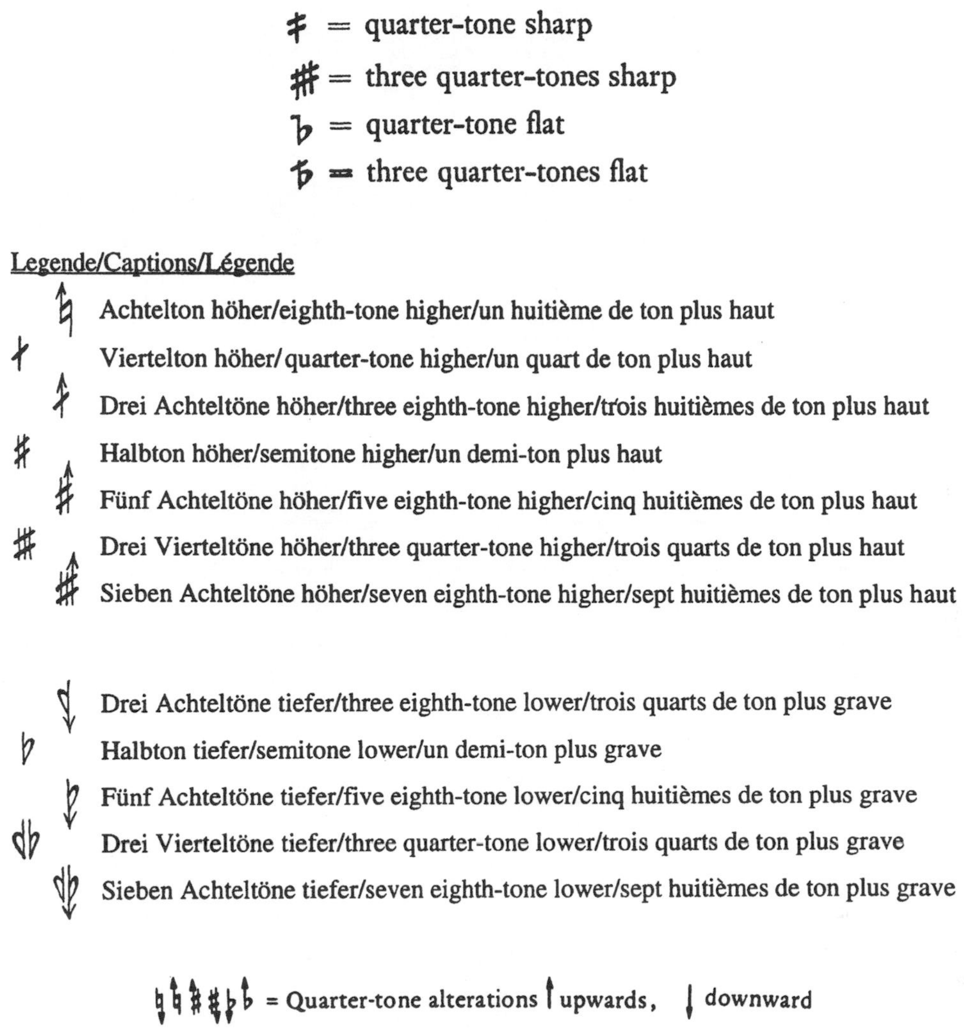

$\sharp$ = quarter-tone sharp

$\sharp\!\!\sharp$ = three quarter-tones sharp

$\flat$ = quarter-tone flat

$\flat$ = three quarter-tones flat

Legende/Captions/Légende

Achtelton höher/eighth-tone higher/un huitième de ton plus haut

Viertelton höher/quarter-tone higher/un quart de ton plus haut

Drei Achteltöne höher/three eighth-tone higher/trois huitièmes de ton plus haut

Halbton höher/semitone higher/un demi-ton plus haut

Fünf Achteltöne höher/five eighth-tone higher/cinq huitièmes de ton plus haut

Drei Vierteltöne höher/three quarter-tone higher/trois quarts de ton plus haut

Sieben Achteltöne höher/seven eighth-tone higher/sept huitièmes de ton plus haut

Drei Achteltöne tiefer/three eighth-tone lower/trois quarts de ton plus grave

Halbton tiefer/semitone lower/un demi-ton plus grave

Fünf Achteltöne tiefer/five eighth-tone lower/cinq huitièmes de ton plus grave

Drei Vierteltöne tiefer/three quarter-tone lower/trois quarts de ton plus grave

Sieben Achteltöne tiefer/seven eighth-tone lower/sept huitièmes de ton plus grave

♮♭♯♯♭♭ = Quarter-tone alterations ↑ upwards, ↓ downward

Figure 2-17   Three approaches to quarter-tone notation: (a) Bartolozzi, (b) Veale, and (c) Wildberger

the key, raising the pitch gradually. This is the technique used in the passage from Penderecki's *Cappriccio* shown in figure 2-20. Penderecki asks the oboist to go just over the break in the upper register to the $C\sharp_6$. This can be achieved by using a trill fingering to play a $C\sharp$ with the first finger of the right hand (see figure 2-21). It is easier to achieve an upward gliss than a downward gliss because it is easier to gradually remove fingers from the holes and keys than it is to gradually cover and lower the keys. Ascending glissandi tend to sound convincing, whereas descending glissandi can sometimes sound "note-y."

While true glissandi are difficult to produce well on the oboe, pitch bends are easy to produce due to the nature of the reed and the embouchure. In most registers it is easy to bend the pitch down at least a semi-tone. This is achieved by relaxing the embouchure and/or pulling the reed out of the mouth slightly. This is most effective in the moderate to high range

Figure 2-18   Ben Johnston's notation of 43-tone scale

(G₅ to F₆) and least effective in the extreme low range (below E₄). The extreme high range (above F₆) can be effective, but these notes are unstable and might crack.

It is possible to bend a pitch up a semi-tone by tightening the embouchure and/or putting more reed in the mouth (also by sliding off the hole when possible). Oboists are more limited in bending the pitch upwards than in bending it downwards. Once again, the extreme high and low ranges present the greatest difficulties.

Jack Vees's *Tattooed Barbie* employs both upper- and lower-pitch bends effectively (see figure 2-22). The composer has indicated that he wants the oboe to sound like a lead rock and roll electric guitar when playing this section, and the oboist plays through a guitar effects box that alters and distorts the oboe sound. By his use of graphic notation, the composer leaves the specific degree of bend up to the individual player. In the performance of this piece, I use both pitch bends and glissandi for the greatest flexibility, smoothness, and amount of pitch change.

In *Byzantium*, Christos Hatzis treats the pitch bend as an ornament (see figure 2-23). He has indicated that he wants exactly a whole step bend. This is possible to achieve in the moderately high register. He has chosen a good note, the high C♯, for this effect. It would be harder one octave lower and virtually impossible two octaves lower.

In the fifth movement of George Crumb's *Ancient Voices of Children*, the oboist is asked to play a passage "timidly, with a sense of loneliness," as shown in figure 2-24. The pitch bends used here create a forlorn sigh, and the composer's indication of rubato and ritard helps the oboist get the most out of this simple gesture. Crumb also wrote this phrase in the best register to achieve this effect.

In improvisational performances, I have sometimes mixed glissandi, pitch bends, and flutter tongue. This produces a very distorted sound but an effective gliss. A straight line that links the starting pitch and ending pitch is the standard notation for glissandi (e.g., Penderecki's *Capriccio*). Pitch bends are also indicated with ascending or descending lines to the desired pitch (e.g., Hatzis's *Byzantium*) or simply with a line indicating the general direction (e.g., Vees's *Tattooed Barbie*).

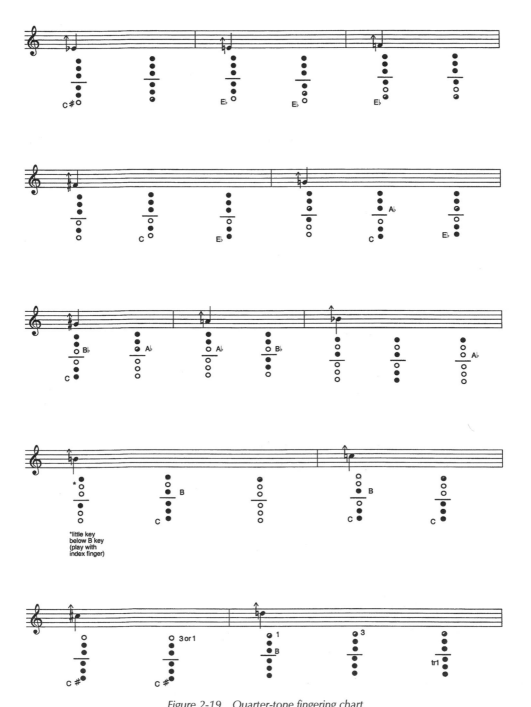

Figure 2-19 Quarter-tone fingering chart

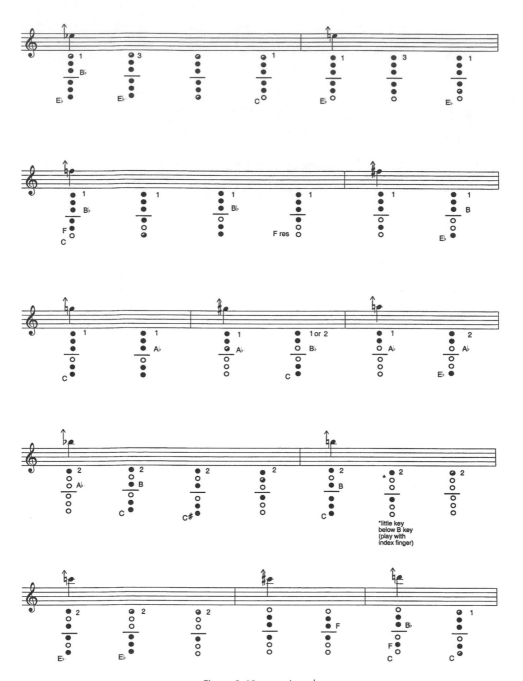

Figure 2-19   continued

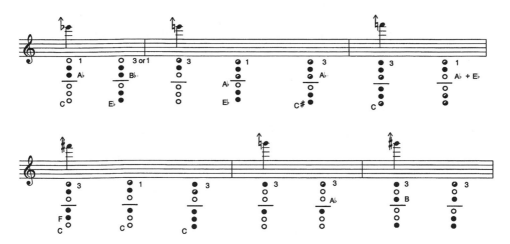

Figure 2-19   continued

Figure 2-20   Penderecki, Capriccio

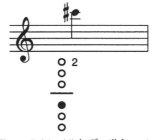

Figure 2-21   High C♯ trill fingering

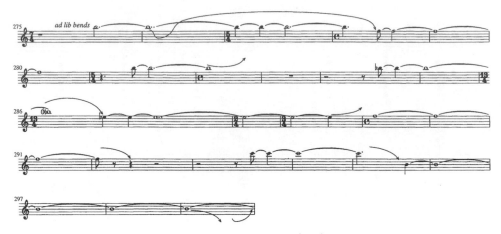

Figure 2-22   Vees, Tattooed Barbie

Figure 2-23   Hatzis, Byzantium

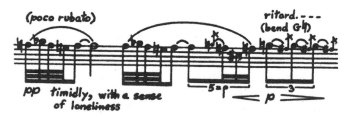

Figure 2-24   Crumb, Ancient Voices of Children

Glissandi

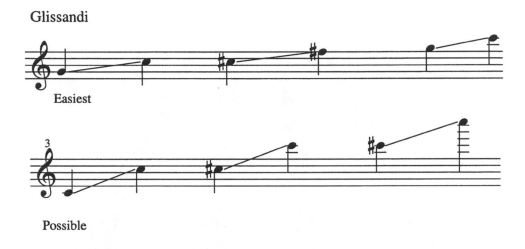

Easiest

Possible

Pitch Bends

It is easiest to bend a semitone down.

Figure 2-25   Chart of glissandi and pitch bends

Indications above regarding glissandi and pitch bends are generally applicable to the English horn and oboe d'amore. Because of the covered hole on the G key, smooth glissandi from a fingered G to A are more difficult than on the oboe. See figure 2-25 for a chart of glissandi and pitch bends.

Upper-Register Fingerings

Composers who explore the oboe stratosphere must proceed with caution! Extremely high notes (e.g., Bb_6 or higher) are often unstable with respect to attack and intonation, and their timbre is almost never full and resonant. Many instruments and the human voice sound louder and more strident in the upper register, but the oboe tends to be quieter and thinner in the upper register. I have often been frustrated by passages that culminate in a very high note (e.g., A_6 or higher) when the composer clearly hoped to achieve a forceful, heroic, and triumphant effect. It is the acoustical nature of the oboe to sound somewhat unsubstantial in the upper register, and that should be kept in mind when the composer is writing a dazzling climax.

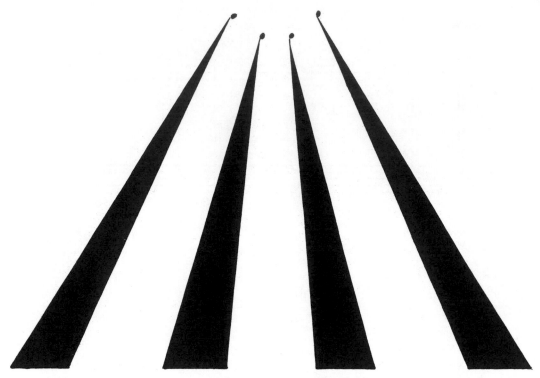

High Notes (courtesy T.J.)

The following list begins with a C♯, the first note that is beyond the range of the octave keys. (Actually, a C♯ is an overblown F♯, a D is an overblown G, etc.) Players may need to put their teeth directly on the reed in order to produce the highest pitches indicated. Not all oboes have a third octave key, but this key is helpful in the execution of some very high notes. If you don't have a third octave key, the first octave key and greater embouchure pressure can be used to execute many of these fingerings.

Musical examples that call for the English horn or oboe d'amore to play above a written G_6 are rare, and it is harder to produce extreme high notes on these instruments than on the oboe. Nevertheless, most of the indicated fingerings are applicable. If a player is having trouble executing high notes on either of the lower horns, it is recommended that he or she try the fingerings on a variety of bocals. Slight variations in the instrument's bore or angle of the bocal make enormous differences in pitch and response. Refer to figure 2-26 for upper-register fingering charts.

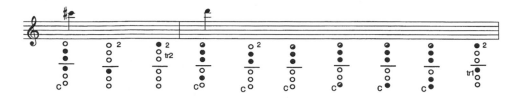

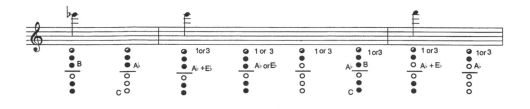

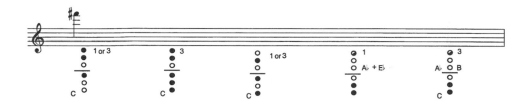

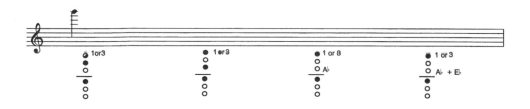

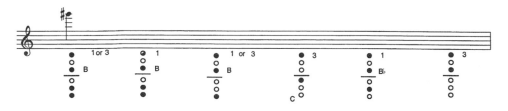

Figure 2-26   Upper-register fingering charts

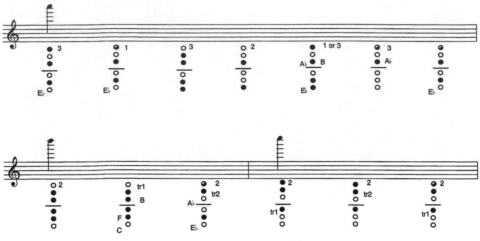

Figure 2-26   continued

Notes

1. Listen to Vees's *Apocrypha* on the enclosed CD and follow the score in appendix 2 for an effective musical application of harmonics.

2. A recording of this piece is included on Hovda's CD, *Coastal Traces*, OO Disc #0029.

3. For additional microtonal fingering charts, see Singer's *Metodo per Oboe* or Veale's *The Techniques of Oboe Playing*.

CHAPTER THREE

~

Multiphonic Techniques

The sound of a multiphonic is familiar to all oboists who have taught beginners or can remember their own early faltering attempts to play high notes. It's easy to produce multiphonics on the oboe. All one needs is to play certain high notes with a relaxed embouchure and low air pressure, and multiple sounds result. With the right combination of fingering, lip position, air pressure, and embouchure, the oboe is capable of producing a huge variety of multiphonics.

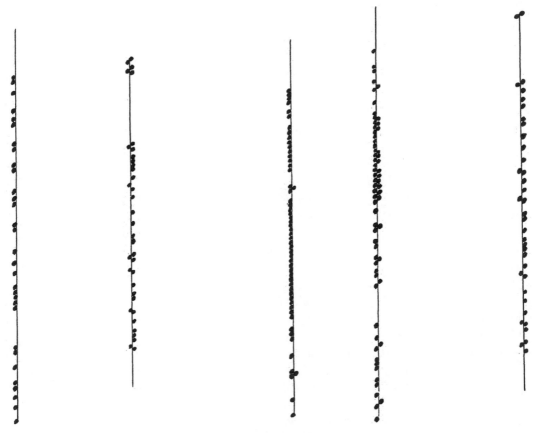

Dense Harmonics (courtesy T.J.)

The fundamental acoustics of the instrument determine the nature of oboe multiphonics and provide a challenge in finding reliable fingerings that work for a range of oboe and reed types. The oboe is basically cone-shaped (similar to a saxophone or bassoon), while the flute and clarinet are basically cylindrical. The mathematical representation of the resonances of a cylindrical system is fairly simple and one-dimensional. Diagrams of this sort of vibrational mode look like sine tones, overlapping at regular and even intervals, comparable to the vibrational mode of a string. In contrast, diagrams of vibrations within a conical system are complex and irregular. It is not surprising, therefore, that oboe multiphonics tend to be dissonant and oddly tuned.

Acoustician Cornelius Nederveen explains, "Frequency, initial transient, stability, ease of blowing and timbre of a note are solely determined by the inner geometry of the entire instrument (including the player's mouth)."[1] Note that the cavity of the reed is included in the overall geometry of the entire instrument. Another acoustician, Arthur Benade, pointed out that even the angle of the cut of a tone hole could affect the sound produced.[2] Hence, the oboe is a complex acoustical system with variables that range from the exact dimensions of inner bores, placement and cut of tone holes, reed types, and even the inner cavity of the individual player's mouth! All of these variables present a challenge in the standardization of reliable fingerings that will work across the range of oboe types, reed types, and players.

The list of multiphonic fingerings below is by no means complete—it does not include the hundreds of fingerings that produce a multiphonic under certain conditions. Instead, I sought to include fingerings that were dependable across a range of oboes and players. These multiphonics are reliable, relatively easy to produce, and stable; they can be played with a broad range of dynamics, can be attacked and tongued easily, and can be played on a variety of instruments and reeds in a variety of climates. Very awkward fingerings were omitted even if they met all of the criteria above. All fingerings were tested by five different oboists who had different oboe types, reed styles, and training.[3] To be included in the list, each fingering needed to work reliably for four out of five of the oboists.[4]

The term "multiphonic" is quite appropriate; the phenomenon is more aptly described as "many sounds" than as a chord. Pitches vary in degrees of intensity, from the very prominent to the barely audible and to difference tones. Timbre varies from raucous conglomerates with lots of beating to delicate wisps; some are highly complex and some are much simpler. Many, if not all, of the pitches tend to deviate from standard tuning. With all these considerations, a notational system that implies a chord is misleading. In the several decades during which multiphonics have been studied, various authors have tried to devise appropriate notational systems, including Singer's proposal of color-coding[5] to Veale's amazingly precise and detailed approach[6] to Holliger's use of a quasi-tablature in which only the oboist's gestures are specified.[7] The system employed here is simpler than Singer's or Veale's; my hope is that it gives enough information while being concise. Conventional notation is used because it is clear and practical, even though it does not always specify exact intonation, dynamic balance, timbre, or complexity. To address this issue, the sound of every multiphonic can be heard on the accompanying CD. Composers and oboists are urged to listen to the CD in order to know more specifically the qualities of each multiphonic.

My system usually lists only the three most prominent pitches. More subtle pitches are almost always present, but they have not been included in the interest of clarity. Many variables affect exact microtonal intonation: each individual's embouchure and lip position on the reed, differences between instruments, and the variable heights of keys. The oboists who tested the fingerings frequently reported slight differences, particularly in the lowest pitch. Because of these variables, I have simply included arrows indicating the general direction of pitches. Graphic symbols indicating lip position on the reed, amount of air pressure, and amount of lip pressure are given only for fingerings that deviate from standard technique. The key at the back of the book explains all symbols. Multiphonics are listed chromatically from the lowest prominent pitch to the highest. Remember that the lowest pitch might not be the most prominent within any specific multiphonic and that difference tones are often present, producing tones even lower than the bottom prominent pitch indicated.

Chenna and Salmi's book, *The Contemporary Oboe*, mentions a fascinating study on perception that was conducted by IRCAM.[8] Six professional musicians were given a multiphonic dictation, and the results varied widely (see figure 3-1). This is an illustration of how highly

multiphonic   results

Figure 3-1   Multiphonic dictation

trained professionals can perceive the same combination of tones in strikingly different ways. I have tested hundreds of fingerings, some of which have been analyzed using sophisticated digital techniques, and very often the resulting pitches seemed different from ones indicated on the fingering chart. Thus, even the most highly refined notational system is open to interpretation.

Four categories of multiphonics are included: (1) the standard complex multiphonic; (2) beating multiphonics, which include two prominent adjacent pitches that cause a beating effect; (3) double harmonics; and (4) metamorphic multiphonics, ones that can smoothly transform from a standard tone into a multiphonic or vice versa.

Most reliable multiphonics can be performed with the same level of artistic sensitivity as any other oboe tone (e.g., with a variable dynamic range including crescendos and diminuendos, all speeds of vibrato, relatively easy progression from one sound to the next, and appropriate trills, double trills, and tremolos). It is impossible to alter the pitch of a single tone within the multiphonic, and the possibility of pitch bends of the entire multiphonic should not be assumed. However, it is possible to alter the speed of the beats in some beating multiphonics by adjusting the embouchure: a relaxed embouchure will produce slower beats and a tighter embouchure will produce faster beats. Many multiphonics can be slightly altered by raising or depressing adjacent keys. Oboists are encouraged to use the chart as a point of departure and to experiment on their own with slightly different fingerings, air pressures, and embouchure positions.

I squandered a significant part of my wasted youth searching for the perfect reed to execute multiphonics and other extended techniques. A very hard reed is good for some raucous multiphonics, and a reed with a long and finely graded tip is better for some more delicate ones. Finally, I realized (with apologies to Gertrude Stein) that "a good reed is a good reed is a good reed." More specifically, it seems that a well-balanced, stable, flexible reed—for example, one that might be used for the performance of Classical-era chamber music—is the type that works best for multiphonics and most extended techniques. I don't think that there's any magic formula for a perfect contemporary music reed—although for extended techniques as well as for standard playing, the reed should correspond to the demands of the piece. If lots of loud beating multiphonics are called for, a robust reed is desirable. If lots of extreme high notes and double harmonics are called for, a lighter reed might be more appropriate. In general, the embouchure used for multiphonics is somewhat more relaxed than the standard embouchure, and the lip position is closer to the string of the reed.

Although multiphonics have been widely used for decades, the notation has not become standardized. The following examples will demonstrate several alternatives for notation in some particularly interesting musical gestures.

Drake Mabry's *Lament for Astralabe* includes a movement, "Chorale," which consists entirely of multiphonics. He notates the entire chord and gives a fingering above every multiphonic, as shown in figure 3-2. This approach is very clear and relatively easy to read. It is

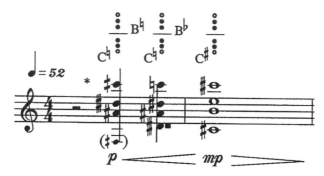

Figure 3-2   Mabry, Lament for Astralabe *(example 1)*

my preferred approach to multiphonic notation for most musical contexts. Mabry's chosen multiphonics sound a lot like the chords he writes, but this is not always the case. One problem with this approach to notation is that the sound of the multiphonic is sometimes so divergent from its appearance that it is confusing for the player. Mabry, an accomplished oboist as well as a composer, wisely notes in the piece's instructions that the work was written for a Lorée oboe and that some modification of fingerings might be necessary for other oboes. As discussed above, multiphonics that work on some makes of oboes do not work on others. For example, I can play Mabry's "Chorale" with the notated fingerings on my Lorée oboe, but not on my Laubin.

The "Chorale" includes ingenious multiphonic writing (see figure 3-3). Mabry juxtaposes dynamics in the grace note figures. The multiphonics he suggests make it easy to execute this passage: the mezzo forte multiphonic is naturally loud, and the piano multiphonic is naturally soft. The last multiphonic is later transformed with a microtonal trill. Mabry indicates that the player should open and close the indicated key (in this case, the "d" key). The gesture concludes with a grand fortissimo on a multiphonic that is naturally loud and raucous.

The excerpt in figure 3-4, from Heinz Holliger's *Studie über Mehrklänge* (chordal study), employs an ingenious approach to notation. This quasi-tablature shows the standard oboe

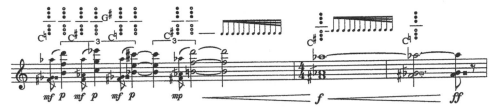

Figure 3-3   Mabry, Lament for Astralabe *(example 2)*

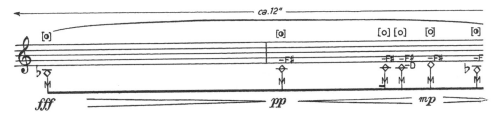

Figure 3-4   Holliger, Studie über Mehrklänge

note (indicated with a diamond notehead) with alterations given above. For example, in the gesture shown, the oboist would finger a low B♭ and open the half hole on the B key. In the next measure, the low C is fingered, and the F♯ is lifted along with the half hole. The next two multiphonics are produced by completely opening the half hole, then lifting the D key as well—and so on. Later in the piece, many techniques are applied to the multiphonics such as tremolo, trill, double trill, glissando, flutter tongue, double tongue, and circular breathing.

An advantage of this type of notation is that most oboists could sight-read it with ease. Chenna and Salmi, in *The Contemporary Oboe*, argue that multiphonics are more accurately thought of as timbral transformations rather than chords, so "it is no longer necessary to notate the presumed multiphonic sounds played."[9] Certainly this notation is clear, easy to read, and practical; however, a disadvantage is that players have no idea what sound is desired if the proposed fingering does not work on their instruments. Given the variables described earlier in this chapter, this is a very real possibility.

Elliott Carter's *Inner Song* includes a multiphonic for which he gives both Holliger's and the more conventional notation (see figure 3-5). It is clear, and there should be no question about what he wants. Another multiphonic (a double harmonic) is shown with only the conventional notation, as shown in figure 3-6.

Vinko Globokar, a remarkably inventive composer who has been at the forefront of the exploration of new instrumental techniques, proposes an entirely different approach to notation in his piece *Discours III*, for five oboes. He indicates the desired prominent pitch and the level of multiphonic complexity with a number above the notehead (see figures 3-7 and 3-8). Globokar has explained to me that he believes players should have the freedom to select the multiphonic that works best for their individual setups, and that by this point, there is enough information on fingerings available so that any resourceful player can come up with the appropriate multiphonics. Globokar's approach is practical, clear, and respectful of the integrity of the individual performer. He leaves a little to chance; however, most performances are proba-

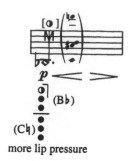

more lip pressure

Figure 3-5   Carter, Inner Song

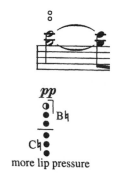

more lip pressure

Figure 3-6   Carter, Inner Song

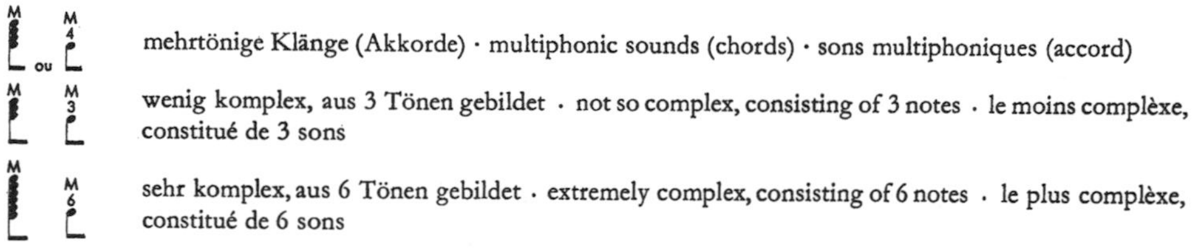

mehrtönige Klänge (Akkorde) · multiphonic sounds (chords) · sons multiphoniques (accord)

wenig komplex, aus 3 Tönen gebildet · not so complex, consisting of 3 notes · le moins complèxe, constitué de 3 sons

sehr komplex, aus 6 Tönen gebildet · extremely complex, consisting of 6 notes · le plus complèxe, constitué de 6 sons

Figure 3-7   Globokar, Discours III

bly closer to his original intention than they would be if he proposed specific fingerings that didn't work for many instrumentalists. Globokar's notation suggests that certain parameters of multiphonics can be indicated (i.e., prominent pitch and level of complexity), but that precise and exact sounds cannot always be relied upon—a very practical approach.

George Brunner's *Teaching No Talking* for oboe and tape, based on a text from the *Tao Te Ching*, includes an expressive gesture in which a single low E♭ transforms into a multiphonic progression and finally dissolves into a high E♭. The composer suggests fingerings in the introduction, and simply uses graphic notation to indicate the two multiphonics (see figure 3-9). This notation is clear, and most players should be able to execute the phrase comfortably.

Another effective use of multiphonics can be found in Ronald Roseman's *Partita for Solo Oboe*. He indicates a multiphonic by using a diamond notehead and writes verbal instructions

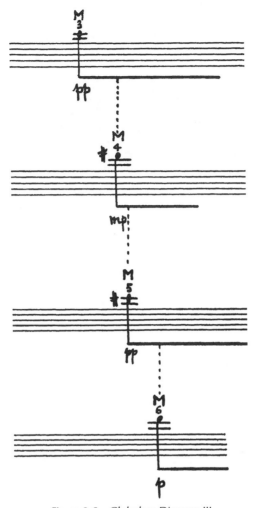

Figure 3-8   Globokar, Discours III

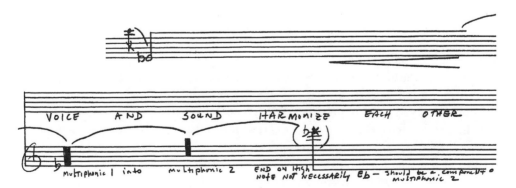

Figure 3-9   Brunner, Teaching No Talking

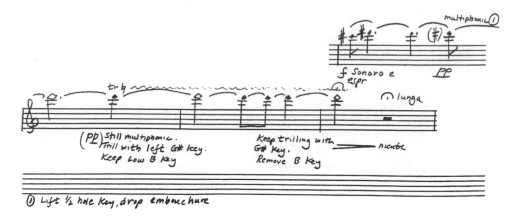

Figure 3-10   Roseman, Partita

regarding performance technique, as shown in figure 3-10. Roseman, a master oboist as well as composer, has chosen a multiphonic that is reliable on every oboe that I know. It's the sound described in the first paragraph of this chapter, the unintentional multiphonic that results (mostly) from using a relaxed embouchure for a high note. This multiphonic is easily trilled, and the pitch of the entire multiphonic is subtly lowered during the trill by lifting the B key. Roseman's notation is clear, effective, and easy to read.

Jack Vees asked me for various combinations of fingerings that could be played with lightning speed for a section of *Tattooed Barbie*. He liked combinations that included occasional

Figure 3-11   Vees, Tattooed Barbie

multiphonics. The passage in figure 3-11 is an excerpt of a section that is performed through a digital delay, accompanied by an extremely distorted 12-string guitar and manic computer-driven drumming. The resulting melange, heard on the accompanying CD track 34, is the chaotic mix the composer desired. This passage is noteworthy (not to mention note-y!) because the multiphonics fly by without delicate embouchure or air-pressure preparation. In this situation, the composer indicates exact fingerings, and there is no other convenient way to execute the passage. If a certain fingering combination doesn't produce a multiphonic or produces a sound different from what is notated, it probably wouldn't significantly alter the desired final effect: a wall of frenetic sound.

Scott Lindroth's *Terza Rima*, for oboe and live interactive electronics, includes a passage in which a multiphonic emerges from a very strong and sweeping electronic gesture (see figure 3-12). The specific multiphonics were chosen for their particularly consonant quality, and they flow almost like a chord progression. (At the recording session, the composer was amazed when I added vibrato to this passage. Why not? Multiphonics are music!) As stated in the

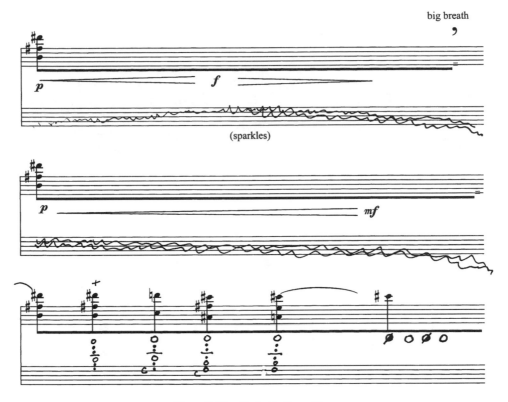

Figure 3-12 Lindroth, Terza Rima

paragraphs above, most stable multiphonics can be treated as any other musical gesture. Vibrato can subtly color a multiphonic just like any other long tone. The last fingering of the example needs only a slight addition of lip pressure to transform into the high C♯, which is then altered with a timbral trill. This excerpt is on CD track 33.

Roger Reynolds includes a number of multiphonic trills in his *Summer Island,* as shown in figure 3-13. His instructions note that *trir* indicates an irregular trill. He uses the conventional notation along with suggested fingerings for these stable and reliable multiphonics. With a sensible combination of fingerings, trills are easily executed on most stable multiphonics.

John Corigliano's *Concerto for Oboe and Orchestra* includes an excellent example of a beating multiphonic. The piece begins with a humorous quasi-tuning of the entire orchestra. The soloist enters with quarter-tone bends and eventually emerges playing a somewhat demented tune that highlights the beating multiphonic centered around A and B♭ (see figure 3-14). I have been seated next to oboists in my local orchestras who quoted this passage during tuning. It was the big inside joke for years after Corigliano's concerto was written.

Luciano Berio's *Sequenza VII* includes a poignant moment when a multiphonic emerges from a single tone, as shown in figure 3-15. Similar to the example Ronald Roseman used, this metamorphic multiphonic is derived from relaxing the lip pressure on a high note and is fairly reliable for most oboists and most oboes. The piece concludes with another gesture in which a single tone and a multiphonic are linked; however, this one does not have the seamless

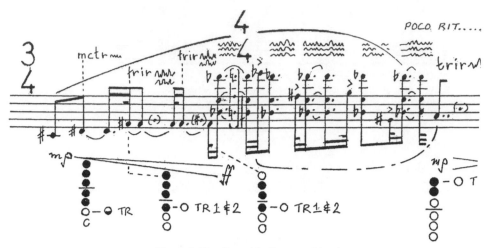

Figure 3-13   Reynolds, Summer Island

Figure 3-14   Corigliano, Oboe Concerto

ppp

Figure 3-15   Berio, Sequenza VII

quality that occurs when the fingering stays the same and only embouchure or air pressure changes. Nevertheless, this example shows the flexibility of multiphonics: it is approached by the C harmonic, the same C is prominent in the multiphonic, and the alternative fingering that Berio suggests for the last C helps to produce the ethereal *ppp* tone required (see figure 3-16).

Berio's piece makes wide use of a particular kind of multiphonic, the double harmonic. This delicate sound is produced by slightly adjusting the fingering, air pressure, and embouchure for a standard harmonic. The interval of a fifth results. Many double harmonics are very difficult to produce and can only be played at a pianissimo dynamic. The *Sequenza* and many

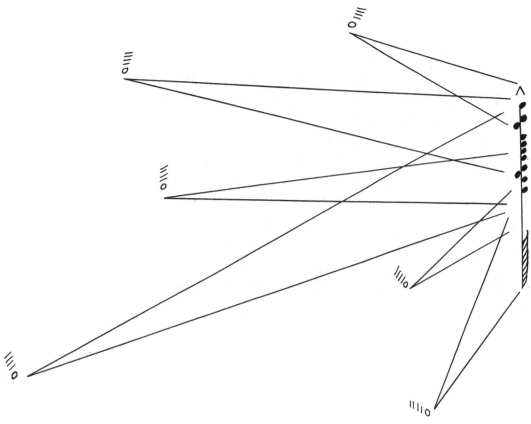

Dramatic Moment (courtesy T.J.)

of the other early pieces that used double harmonics were written for Heinz Holliger who plays a Rigoutat oboe. The Rigoutat oboe differs from many others in the design of the hole under the B key. This key is always half open for double harmonic fingerings; and, accordingly, the double harmonics are easier to produce on a Rigoutat. Double harmonics can be produced with other types of oboe, but they are less flexible and more difficult to play. Berio sometimes lets a double harmonic stand alone (figure 3-17), sometimes adds a trill or double trill (figure 3-18), and sometimes approaches it from one of the component notes (figure 3-19).

Notation of double harmonics is standardized and is demonstrated by the Berio excerpt above. The two small circles are placed above the pitches that are to be heard.

All of the previous musical examples were written either by accomplished composer-oboists or by composers who collaborated closely with oboists. As mentioned in chapter 1, it is highly recommended that composers work directly with a living, breathing, squawking oboist when writing extended technique passages, especially multiphonics. Even the most reliable fingerings will sometimes produce surprising results or unexpected challenges for the performer.

Figures 3-20 and 3-21 provide fingering charts for both standard and beating multiphonics. As indicated earlier, double harmonics are sometimes rather difficult to produce. Figure 3-22 gives the standard fingerings and alternatives that have been proposed by James Ostryniec. I include some fingerings that, while not reliable for every instrument, do work well in some cases.

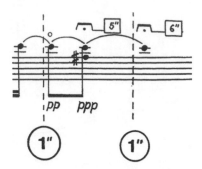

Figure 3-16 *Berio,* Sequenza VII

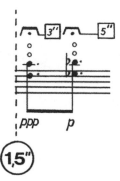

Figure 3-17 *Berio,* Sequenza VII

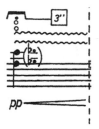

Figure 3-18 *Berio,* Sequenza VII

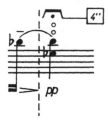

Figure 3-19 *Berio,* Sequenza VII

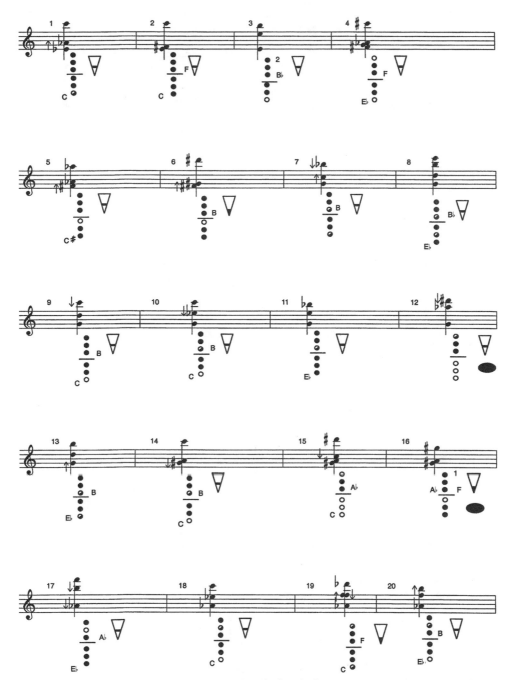

Figure 3-20   Standard multiphonics

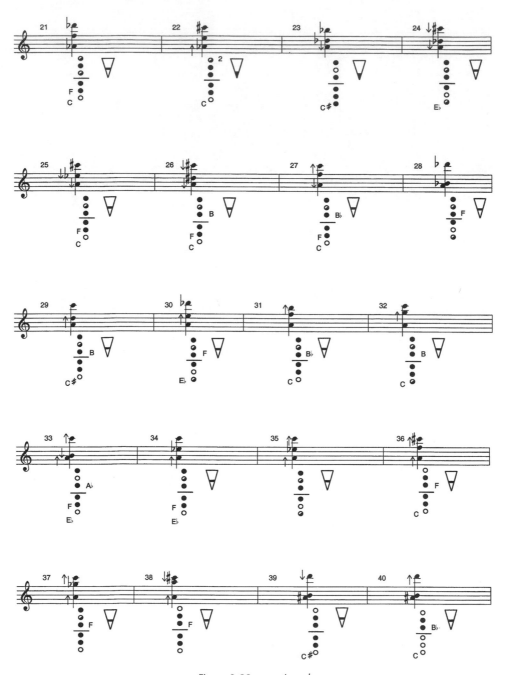

Figure 3-20   continued

Figure 3-20   continued

Figure 3-20   continued

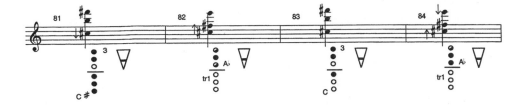

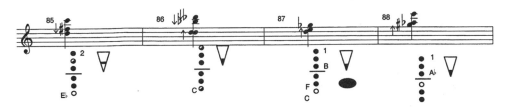

Figure 3-20   continued

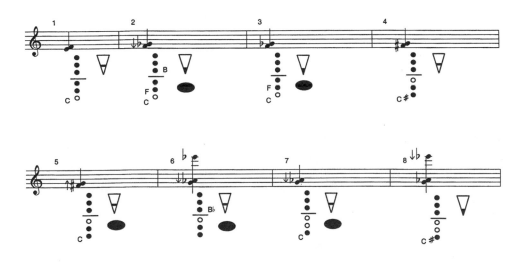

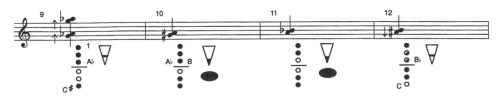

Figure 3-21   Beating multiphonics

Figure 3-21   continued

Figure 3-21   continued

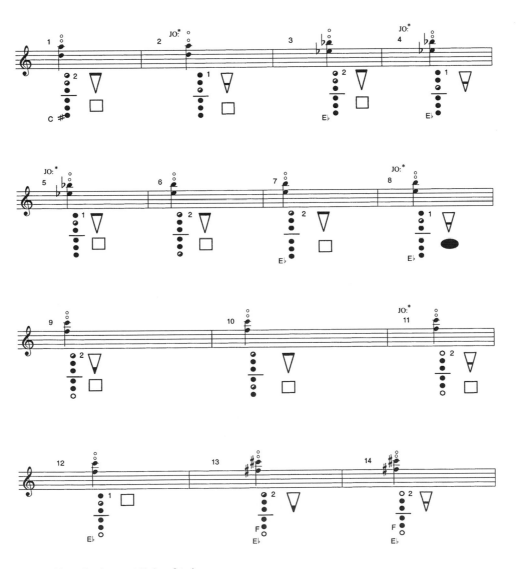

*alternate fingerings suggested by James Ostryniec

Figure 3-22   Double harmonics

Many multiphonics can metamorphose into and out of a single tone with subtle changes of embouchure or air pressure. Here are a few of my most reliable favorites:

Category 1. Most notes above the C_6 can easily transform into a multiphonic with a simple change in lip pressure or reed position.

Category 2. Many beating multiphonics can emerge from the lowest pitch if the oboist plays on the extreme tip of the reed with light air pressure. Note that as the multiphonic emerges, the player can control the speed of the beating.

Category 3. This is just a sample of many possibilities. Included are fingerings that flexibly transform from a low pitch to the multiphonic and then into a high pitch. One could also play from the higher pitch to the lower pitch. Players are encouraged to experiment with lip pressures and reed positions to find other fingerings that work for their setup.

Figure 3-23 provides fingering charts for metamorphic multiphonics.

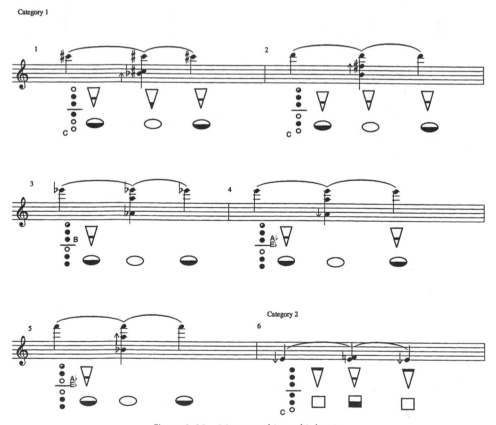

Figure 3-23   Metamorphic multiphonics

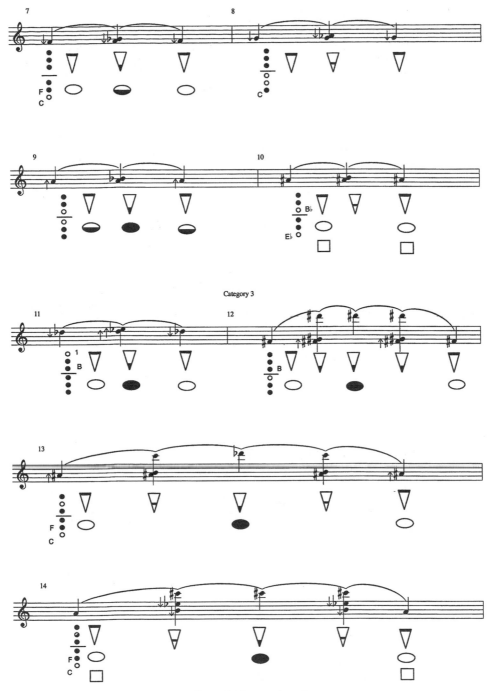

Figure 3-23   continued

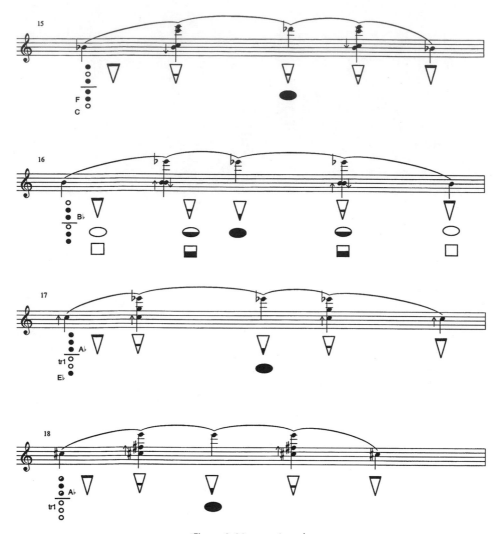

Figure 3-23   continued

Notes

1. Cornelius Nederveen, *Acoustical Aspects of Woodwind Instruments* (Amsterdam: Frits Knur, 1969), 97.

2. Arthur Benade, *Fundamentals of Musical Acoustics* (New York: Oxford University Press, 1976), 7501.

3. The testers were myself on Laubin and Lorée, Jacqueline LeClaire and Jenny Raymond on Lorée, Electra Reed O'Mara on Marigaux, and Judi Scramlin on Rigoutat.

4. For those intrepid souls who want a larger list of multiphonics, refer to Andrea Chenna with Massimiliano Salmi and Omar Zoboli, *Manuale Dell'Oboe Contemporaneo* [The Contemporary Oboe] (Milan: Rugginenti Editore, 1994); Lawrence Singer and Bruno Bartolozzi, *Metodo per Oboe* (Milan: Edizioni Suvini Zerboni, 1969); or Peter Veale and Claus-Steffen Mahnkopf, *The Techniques of Oboe Playing* (Basel, Switzerland: Barenreiter Kassel, 1994).

5. Lawrence Singer, "Woodwind Development; A Monophonic and Multiphonic Point of View," *Woodwind World* 14 (June 1975): 14.

6. Veale and Mahnkopf. *The Techniques of Oboe Playing*, 75–123.

7. Heinz Holliger, ed., *Pro Musica Nova, Studies for Playing Avant-garde Music for the Oboe* (Wiesbaden, Germany: Breitkopf & Hartel, 1972), 42–45.

8. Chenna, Salmi, and Zoboli, *Manuale Dell'Oboe Contemporaneo*, 25.

9. Chenna, Salmi, and Zoboli, *Manuale Dell'Oboe Contemporaneo*.

CHAPTER FOUR

Other Resources

This chapter includes directions for the performance of miscellaneous techniques including tricky trills, double trills, microtonal trills, tremolos, articulations, timbral modifications using vibrato or rolling tone, singing and playing, and other resources.

Trills

Tricky Trills

Figure 4-1 shows a fingering chart for standard trills that require fingerings that aren't immediately obvious. Although these combinations are well known to some players, there are a number of fairly sophisticated oboists who aren't aware of all of this information. These fingerings apply to all instruments in the oboe family.

Double Trills

A double trill is executed by alternating between fingers on the left and right hands or the first and second fingers of the right hand. It is a standard trill, but it can be played with far greater speed. Double trills are not available on every pitch throughout the instrument; they can only be played on the pitches notated in the fingering chart in figure 4-2. Nevertheless, it is an extremely effective technique that is easy to produce on the available pitches. One can also execute a double trill between harmonics or between multiphonics. Other techniques such as flutter tongue or glissando can be applied to a double trill. The notation for a double trill is standardized, a trill marking with two wavy lines (see figure 4-2).

Penderecki's extraordinary and colorful *Capriccio for Oboe and 11 Strings* includes a passage with a succession of double trills, as shown in figure 4-3. Accompanied by strings trilling a chord cluster, this gesture begins quietly and subtly, and grows to a noisy frenzy, displaying some of the versatility of double trills.

Jack Vees's *Apocrypha* for oboe and tape uses double trills slurred to harmonic double trills (see figure 4-4). One of the apocryphal acts the performer commits in this piece would impress a ventriloquist: the live performer slurs to the related harmonic while the loudspeaker elsewhere in the performance space continues the original notes.

In the passage from *Lament for Astralabe* shown in figure 4-5, Drake Mabry asks the player to start the double trill, then to raise and lower other keys and to apply breath accents while

55

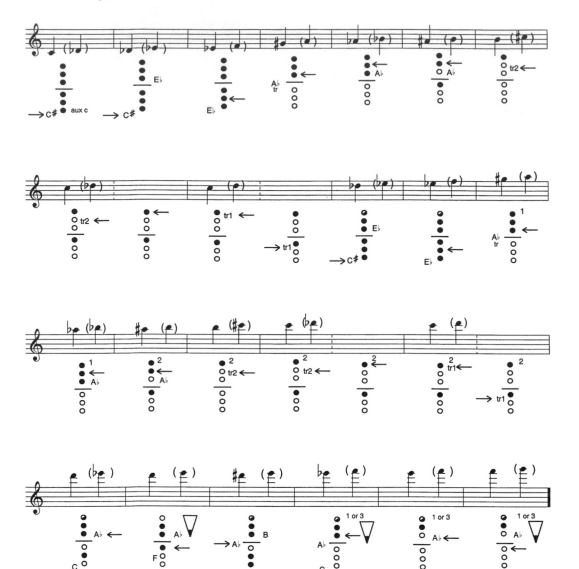

Figure 4-1   Tricky trill fingerings

the trill is progressing. This creates a dramatic microtonal percolation, ever more lively and varied, even though the pitch ranges only between an A and a C.

Ronald Caltabiano's *Sonata* for English horn includes a brief gesture with a double trill that includes four separate pitches (see figure 4-6). The F# key is trilled, and the A key is opened and closed to achieve irregular iterations of A, B♭, B, and C. This is the same fingering combination used in the Mabry example above, except that it is not microtonal because the G# key is left alone. All the double trills listed below are available and easy to produce on the English horn and oboe d'amore. The chart indicates the written pitches, not the sounding pitches.

Krenek's *Four Pieces* includes double trills with interesting modifications: in Piece 2 he

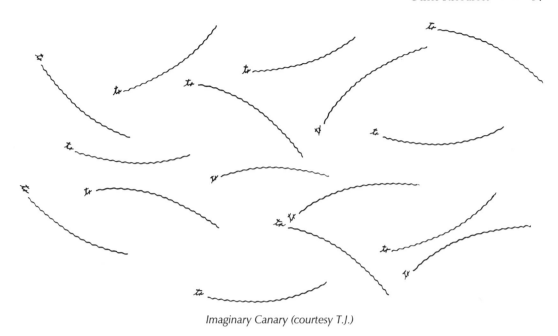

Imaginary Canary (courtesy T.J.)

Figure 4-2   Double trill notation (Krenek, piece 2, measures 19–20)

Figure 4-3   Penderecki, Capriccio

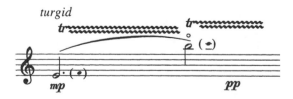

Figure 4-4   Vees, Apocrypha, first measure of Turgid, page 2

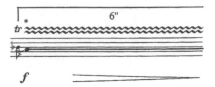

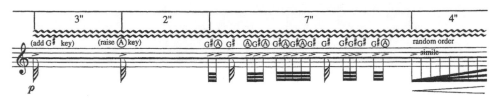

Figure 4-5   Mabry, Lament for Astralabe, page 4, 3rd and 4th systems

Figure 4-6   Caltabiano, Sonata, measure 94

Figure 4-7   Krenek, Four Pieces, piece 2, measure 3; piece 4, measures 6–7

includes a double trill with a flutter tongue, and in Piece 4 he asks the oboist to gliss while trilling (see figure 4-7). Note that this passage can be fairly easily executed by gradually sliding the left hand off the keys. Refer to figure 4-8 for a series of double trill charts.

Microtonal Trills

Microtonal trills, also known as unison trills, timbre trills, micro-interval trills, or color trills, are abundant throughout the range of the oboe. I prefer the term "microtonal" because it is the most accurate: if there is a detectable change of timbre, there is almost always at least a

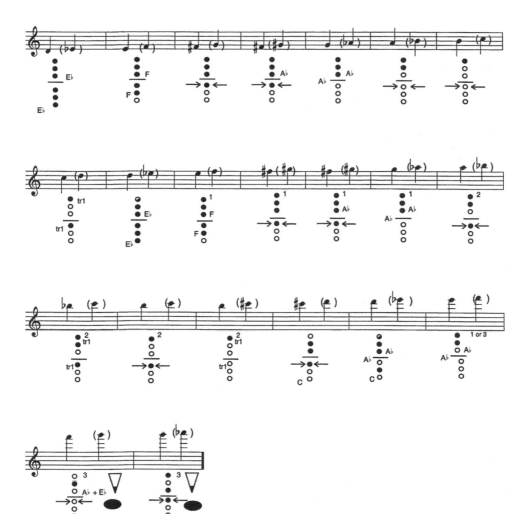

Figure 4-8   Double trill fingering charts

small change in pitch. Many composers have asked for this technique, but few agree on what to call it or how to notate it. In *Dmaathen*, Iannis Xenakis simply writes the words "unison trill" above a note.[1] Ursula Mamlock's *Five Capriccios* include trills that are footnoted with suggested fingerings for a unison trill.[2] In *Distance*, Toru Takemitsu notates a normal trill, but suggests a fingering that produces a micro-interval.[3] Berio indicates micro-interval trills with a wavy line and suggested fingerings in the instructions to *Sequenza VII* (see figure 4-9).

Eleanor Hovda chooses graphic notation and verbal instructions in *Jo Ha Kyu*. As shown in figure 4-10, occasional "flicks" of double tonguing also alter the note. In *Apocrypha*, Jack Vees indicates a standard trill but writes "ttr" (timbre trill) beforehand and includes an explanatory note in his preface (see figure 4-11). He also indicates preferred fingerings, but leaves the final choice to the performer.

In *Summer Island*, Roger Reynolds also uses the standard trill notation, but writes

TRILLER MIT MIKROINTERVALLEN
TRILLS WITH MICROINTERVALS

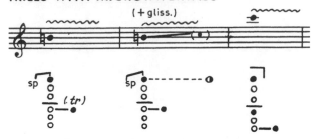

Figure 4-9   Berio, Sequenza, measure 31

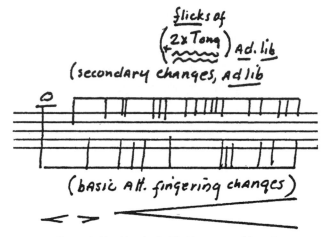

Figure 4-10   Hovda, Jo Ha Kyu, second long B

Figure 4-11   Vees, Apocrypha, page 2, 3rd system

"mctr"(micro-interval trill) beforehand (see figure 4-12). He also includes an explanatory note in his preface. This is my preferred notation because it's easy to tell at a glance that this is a trill, and yet it looks different enough so that one would not mistake it for a standard trill. In *Réflexion*, Shinohara specifies the quarter-tone interval desired (shown in figure 4-13).

Since microtonal trill notation has not become standardized, it is advisable to include an explanatory note in the preface of any composition utilizing this technique. The fingerings in

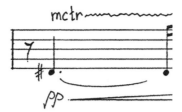

Figure 4-12   D♯ micro-interval trill from the first page of Summer Island

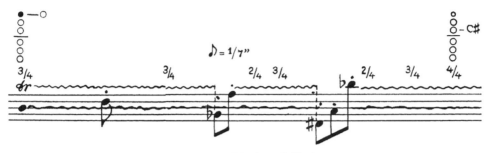

Figure 4-13   Shinohara, Réflexion

figure 4-14 will also apply to the oboe d'amore and English horn, with the exception of those fingerings that utilize the low B♭ key.

Tremolos

A woodwind tremolo is a trill that is bigger than a whole step. It is completely different from the bowed tremolo produced on a stringed instrument (i.e., rapid bowing on a single pitch). Many tremolos are easy for oboists to execute with speed and agility. Some are extremely awkward, including:

- Ones that require the left or right pinkie to slide (e.g., low B♭ to low E♭)
- Ones that require a slide on and off the half-hole key
- Ones that go over the break ($C_5 - C♯_5$ or $C_6 - C♯_6$)
- Many that require some fingers to be depressed when others are lifted

In general, the wider the interval, the slower the tremolo will be; and intervals larger than a sixth are often hard to produce cleanly. Many tremolos can be executed over wide leaps more comfortably by leaving down lower keys that will not strongly affect the pitch of the higher note (e.g., low B♭ to B natural below.) Most tremolos that require movement of the fingers of only one hand will be easier to play very quickly than those that require coordination of both hands. Notation for tremolos is standardized as shown in figure 4-15.

Xenakis includes a phrase that begins with a tremolo in *Dmaathen* (see figure 4-16). If the player keeps the A♭ key depressed, the tremolo can be executed very quickly and the pitch of both notes is true.

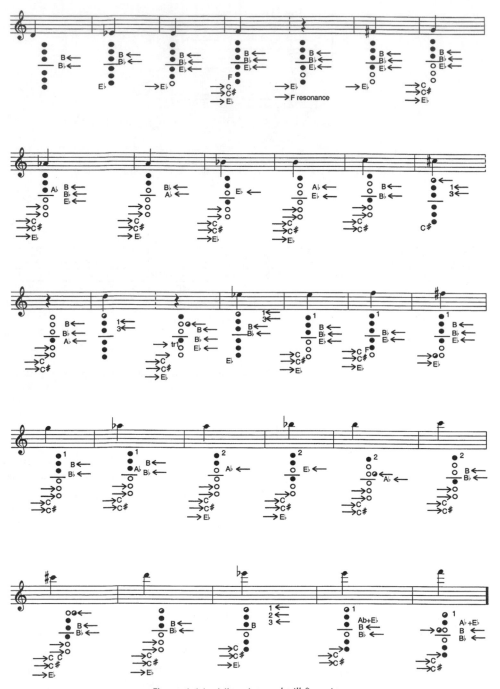

Figure 4-14   Micro-interval trill fingerings

Figure 4-15   Tremolo notation (low C to G)

Figure 4-16   Xenakis, Dmaathen

Figure 4-17   Corigliano, Oboe Concerto (Rheita movement)

Corigliano includes a tremolo in the lively "Rheita" movement of his Oboe Concerto. As shown in figure 4-17, the tremolo is played very briefly and rhythmically, and it functions as an ornament on the fundamental pitch. Note that this tremolo is easy to produce, even though it goes over the break, because the trill fingering can be used for the D♭.

The collection of recommended tremolos in figure 4-18 includes comfortable fingering combinations. Most are highly idiomatic and can be easily executed with lightning speed. Those marked with an "S" (for "slower") are less comfortable, but they still can be executed quite quickly. Extremely awkward combinations are omitted. Some tremolos use alternate fingerings that are very true to the normal timbre and pitch. Other tremolos are available, but not as easy to produce. All these fingerings apply to the oboe d'amore and English horn with the exception of those that utilize the low B♭ key.[4]

Double Tonguing

Double tonguing on the oboe is performed by alternating standard attacks (in which the tip of the tongue comes into direct contact with the reed) with attacks in which the tongue contacts the top palate of the mouth. The syllables that most oboists associate with these two attacks are "te" or "tu" and "ke" or "ku." The challenge in double tonguing is to make the palatal attack as strong as the standard attack. Here are some suggestions for developing a strong double-tonguing technique:

- First, practice only the "ke" attack in the middle register—until it is no longer possible to notice a difference between the "ke" attack and the "te" attack. If you have never double-tongued before, this step may take weeks to perfect.

Figure 4-18   Recommended tremolos fingering chart

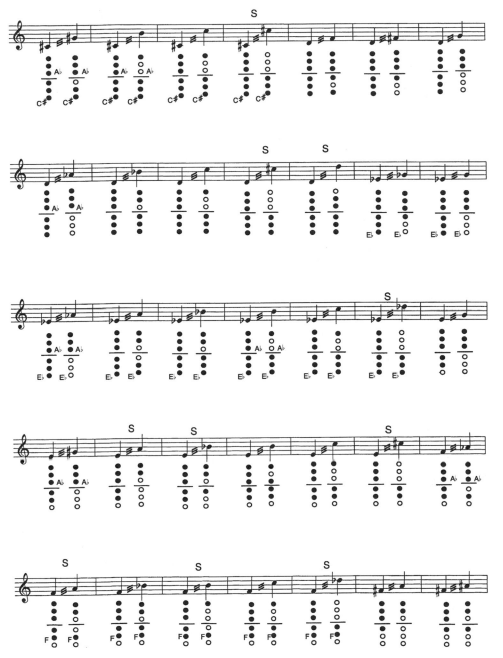

Figure 4-18 continued

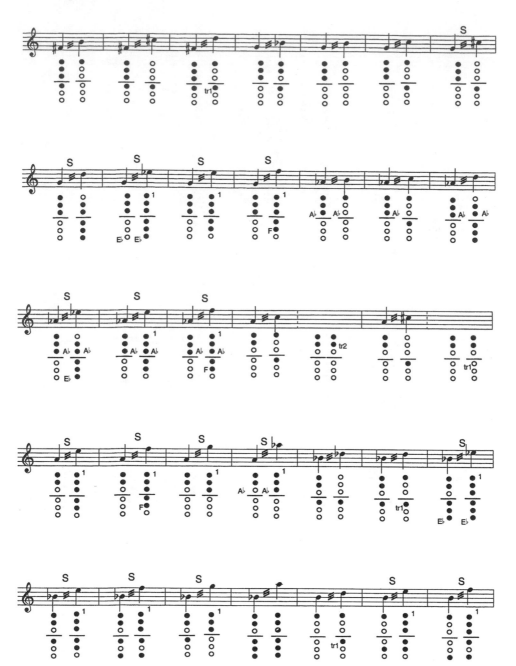

Figure 4-18   continued

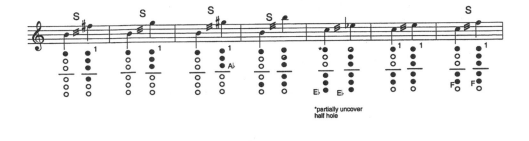

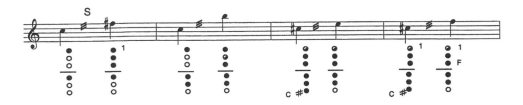

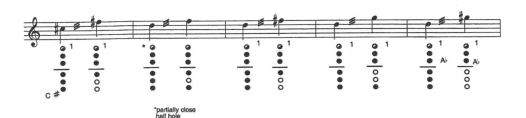

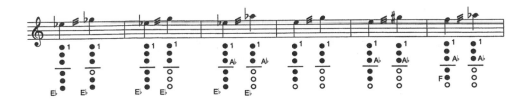

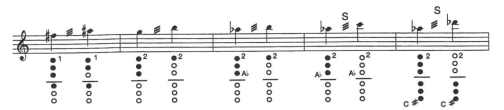

Figure 4-18   continued

- Practice, alternating the "te" and "ke" attacks slowly, on one note in the middle register and with rhythms shown in figure 4-19.
- Practice these rhythms in simple scale patterns.
- Practice in the upper and lower registers.
- Pick excerpts of well-known pieces and practice them alternately with single and double tonguing. Make sure to practice triplet passages so as to emphasize the palatal attack.

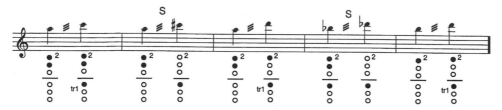

Figure 4-18   continued

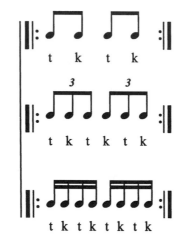

Figure 4-19   Double tonguing exercises

Double tonguing is usually used to achieve faster articulation and is left up to the player's discretion. However, some composers have asked specifically for double tonguing to achieve particular effects. This is often notated simply with a "tktk" before a passage, usually accompanied by an explanatory note. Globokar uses this notation to indicate fleet articulation over a passage of random notes in *Discours III* (see figure 4-20). A live or prerecorded oboist playing a double-tongued gesture on a single note accompanies this. Globokar also requests double-tonguing technique with subtle air pressure so as to produce only the air sound (see figure 4-21).

In *Jo Ha Kyu*, Eleanor Hovda requests a similar technique, although this time with random fingerings and just enough air pressure to produce audible pitches at the quietest possible dynamic level (see figure 4-22). She uses graphic notation and her own unique appellation, "industrials in air," for this lively and subtle gesture (see CD track 35).

Double tonguing can be executed with ease on the English horn and oboe d'amore. Triple

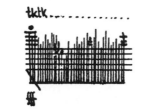

Figure 4-20   Globokar, Discours III

Figure 4-21   Globokar, Discours III

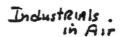

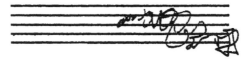

Figure 4-22   Hovda, Jo Ha Kyu, *Industrials section*

tonguing follows the same principle; however, an additional "te" is added, so the pattern is "te ke te—te ke te" and so on.

Flutter Tonguing

Flutter tonguing is more difficult to achieve on the oboe than on many other wind instruments. As recently as 1976, a reputable author wrote that it was impossible on the oboe.[5] Composers should not assume that every oboist can execute a flutter tongue. At the time of this writing, it is not considered standard oboe technique. However, with some determination and practice, most oboists should be able to do it on any of the instruments in the oboe family.

Flutter tonguing is achieved by rolling an "r," either with the tongue or the uvula. The tongued flutter is easier for many oboists, but it has the disadvantage of destabilizing the embouchure, making it difficult to do quietly or in extremes of the upper register. The uvular flutter is probably superior, though it is a much more subtle sound. I think this technique is challenging for English-speaking people because we don't exercise this part of our mouth in everyday language. I discovered, to my great surprise, that my uvular flutter tonguing was enhanced by my study of the German language. When I spent time every day using the back of my throat to produce guttural words, it was much easier to use the uvula for a flutter tongue. The uvular flutter is easier to control in the extremes of dynamics and register.

To develop a tongued flutter, first roll an "r." Next, practice rolling the "r" while blowing out. Practice next by rolling and blowing through a drinking straw into a glass of water. The next step is to roll while blowing through a loose reed away from the instrument. (Try a flexible English horn reed first. The larger size makes the process easier.) Finally, play with the reed on the instrument, starting with the middle register and working outward.

Following is Heinz Holliger's explanation of the uvular flutter-tonguing technique:

> Play a note while articulating a palatal *r* (the tongued *r* is unfavorable, since the reed obstructs the tongue). The palate should be as relaxed as possible, so that the *r* does not change to a fricative *ch* (*x*): you should position your mouth as for the pronunciation of an *O* sound. In order to facilitate the production of the *r*, it is recommended, while practicing, to first press the reed against the upper lip, and then exhale some air (over a looser lower lip). Begin by practicing flutter tonguing on single notes in the middle register (*mf* later, *pp-ff*, cresc.—dim.), then move on to the upper and lower registers. Later, practice flutter tonguing figures of several notes, scales, arpeggios, trills, etc.[6]

Flutter tonguing is sometimes notated by writing the letters "flz" or "flatterz" before a gesture; however, the most conventional notation consists of slash marks through the note stem. Ferneyhough uses this notation, along with "flz," in his *Coloratura*. Note, in figure 4-23, that

Figure 4-23   Ferneyhough, Coloratura

the flutter is applied rhythmically to accent and color the sustained tone. Penderecki uses the notation shown in figure 4-24 in his *Capriccio*.

Figure 4-24   Penderecki, first flutter in Capriccio

In Ronald Roseman's *Partita*, a flutter is indicated with the slash marks and a verbal indication (see figure 4-25). Roseman, an oboist and oboe teacher who knew the limits of many players' technique, suggested an alternative in case the flutter could not be executed, a very practical approach.

Vibrato

Most professional oboists have a refined and varied approach to vibrato. It has become part of standard technique and is easy to produce in all registers and on all instruments in the oboe

Figure 4-25   Roseman, Partita

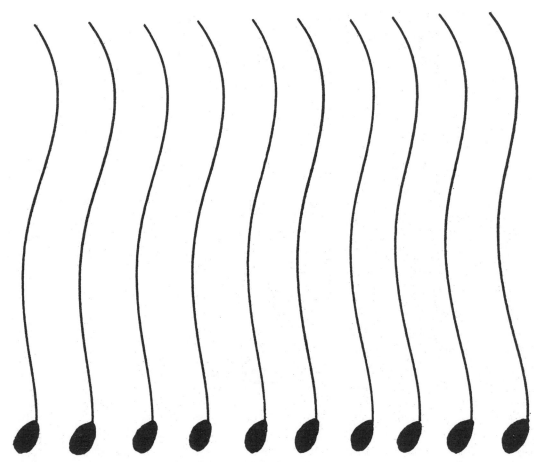

Quarter Notes with Vibrato (courtesy T.J.)

family. Most oboists produce vibrato with movements of the diaphragm, but sometimes the lips or even the jaw can be used for extreme types of vibrato. If the oboe is pulled out of the mouth, the pitch will drop; if it is pushed in, the pitch will raise. If the jaw is opened, the pitch will drop, and if it is closed, the pitch will raise. The speed and the amplitude of the vibrato are variable and independent of each other. The usual tendency is for high notes to have a faster and narrower vibrato, and for lower notes to have a slower and somewhat wider vibrato, but these tendencies are simply a matter of taste. Most oboists can play vibrato with a wide range of speed and amplitude in all registers.

Composers often indicate the absence of vibrato with the initials "NV" (no vibrato, or *non vibrato*). In *Images*, Isang Yun uses n.v., and also p.v. (*poco vibrato*), v. (*vibrato*), and v.p.c. (*vibrato poco a poco*).[7] He also uses a wavy line to indicate a glissando with vibrato and a straight one for a glissando without vibrato. The initials "MV" are often used to indicate *molto vibrato*. Some composers use graphic notation to indicate the amplitude of the vibrato. It is always advisable to explain vibrato notation in the preface to the piece because this is not completely standardized.

Judith Shatin uses both graphic notation and initials to indicate alterations of vibrato in the "Frantic" movement of her *Assembly Line #1*, as shown in figure 4-26.

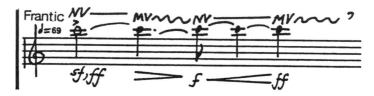

Figure 4-26 Shatin, Assembly Line #1

Breath Accents

Breath accents are executed with a technique identical to diaphragm vibrato. While sustaining a tone, the oboist can isolate a single diaphragm surge, and an accent occurs within the held tone. (The same technique is employed when players put a vibrato spin on the beginning of an accented note.) Breath accents are easy to produce on all instruments in the oboe family and in all registers and dynamic ranges. In the "Mysterious" movement of *Assembly Line #1*, Shatin indicates breath accents with X noteheads in a specific rhythm (see figure 4-27). This

Figure 4-27 Shatin, Assembly Line #1

is clear notation, but it is not standardized and should be explained in a preface to the composition.

Smorzato

The extended techniques pioneer, Bartolozzi, recommended the smorzato sound for all winds, but it is a technique rarely demanded of oboists.[8] It is an abrupt, jerking type of single-stroke vibrato, which is produced by coordinating movements of the jaw with pressure from the lips so as to vary volume without altering pitch.[9] This creates sudden surges in volume. Bartolozzi recommends it in the middle and upper-middle registers and with a dynamic range that does not exceed mezzo forte. He recommends the notation shown in figure 4-28.

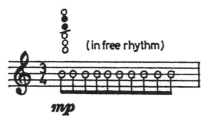

Figure 4-28   *Bartolozzi, from* New Sounds for Woodwind

Rolling Tone

The rolling tone is possible in the lowest range of the oboe (B♭₃ to D₃) and is produced by using extreme lip pressure to make a beating or rolling quality. It is a unique and attractive sound, but it is difficult to control and to play with a wide range of dynamics. It is easiest to produce a rolling tone by increasing the lip pressure after the note has begun, the technique called for in this passage from Denisov's *Solo* (see figure 4-29). It is sometimes difficult to start

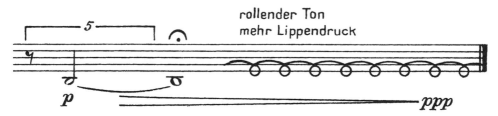

Figure 4-29   *Rolling tone from Denisov,* Solo

a rolling tone precisely, but once it has been established, it is not hard to execute the diminuendo called for here.

The notation for a rolling tone is not standardized, but I recommend the symbol employed by Isang Yun in his solo piece *Piri* (see figure 4-30).

The rolling tone can be executed on the oboe d'amore and English horn. Ingram Marshall calls for one in his *Holy Ghosts*, for oboe d'amore with digital delays. The beating effect of the rolling tone is enhanced by an electronic delay in the phrase shown in figure 4-31.

The ease of producing a rolling tone and its specific range may vary substantially on different instruments and with different reeds. Composers wishing to use this technique would be wise to check it out with their particular performer.

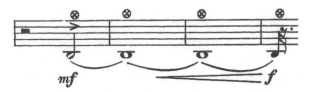

Figure 4-30   Yun, Piri

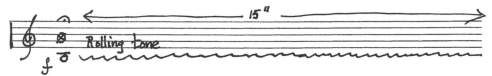

Figure 4-31   Marshall, Holy Ghosts

Singing and Playing Simultaneously

This technique, which produces such a marvelous effect when performed by jazz saxophonists and flutists, is extremely problematic on the oboe. Due to the closed-mouth position and highly focused embouchure, it is almost impossible to produce a strong vocal volume. One might be able to use amplification to remedy this; however, it is also difficult to balance the sung (or, more precisely, hummed) tone and the instrumental tone. In addition, composers should remember that pieces that specify low vocal pitches are impossible for women to perform. (The reverse is not true: men can sing falsetto.) Two notable oboe pieces call for this technique: *Distance* by Takemitsu and *Atemstudie* by Globokar.[10]

Circular Breathing

Circular breathing is a technique used to execute long passages without breaking the wind stream to breathe. Instead, inhalation occurs through the nose while exhalation occurs through the mouth cavity. Non-Western double-reed performers have used the technique for centuries, and many modern oboists use it for long passages, such as Bach obligatos.

Circular breathing at first seems counterintuitive: it's strange to breathe out and in simultaneously, but the technique can easily be developed. First, fill the mouth with air and puff out your cheeks. Then expel the air from your mouth while inhaling through the nose. It might help at first to press it out with both hands on your cheeks. Eventually, practice blowing out using only the cheek muscles and tongue. Chenna and Salmi suggest filling the mouth with water and then expelling a fine stream of water from the mouth while breathing in and out with the nose.[11] Once this becomes comfortable, try the same thing with a drinking straw in a cup of water. Then try it with a reed alone, and finally try it with the reed attached to the instrument. It is easier at first to use a very flexible reed—a big floppy English horn reed is ideal.

Once the basic principle is understood, practice is needed to stabilize the tone, intonation, and dynamics. It's best to start with the middle register and a moderate dynamic level. Because oboe playing requires such a small volume of air, it is advisable to practice both exhaling as well as inhaling through the nose while producing a tone. Until the circular breathing technique is perfected, it is easier to execute it on trills or florid passages because subtle variations in tone are more difficult to hear. Once the technique is developed, it is easily applied to all instruments in the oboe family. Most mere mortals will only be able to sustain circular breathing for a limit of a couple of minutes without needing to relax the embouchure or have a good lungful of fresh air.

In *Jo Ha Kyu*, Eleanor Hovda writes a dazzling passage in which the oboist speeds through a combination of fingerings that, when played with low air pressure and a relaxed embouchure, produce microtones. Gradually the performer increases air pressure and lip pressure, and multiphonics start popping out of the texture. By the end of the gesture, if lots of lip pressure is applied and the lip position slips toward the string of the reed, higher octave multiphonics and notes pop out. This gradual evolution is played without a break as long as possible with one circular breathing inhalation. The composer gives the fingering and uses words and graphic notation to instruct the performer. (Refer to CD track 35.)

In the multiphonic passage described in chapter 3, figure 3-11 (from Jack Vees's *Tattooed Barbie*) the oboist is asked to play the entire three-page passage using the circular breathing technique, if possible. This section, which comes after about eleven minutes of intense playing, lasts just under two minutes, and it pushes me to my limits. Both the musical examples noted include very fast successions of notes, which mask any instability of tone that might be produced by the circular breathing technique.

Miscellaneous Techniques

Overblown Notes
Berio uses the notation in figure 4-32 to indicate a note that is to be overblown.[12] To overblow a note, simply employ greater than usual air pressure. The resulting tone will be somewhat distorted and may sound an octave higher. This technique has the greatest effect on low notes.

Figure 4-32   Berio, Sequenza VII, overblown notation

Muting
A mute is rarely called for, but it can dampen the tone, especially in the lower and middle registers. Usually it is indicated with the standard Italian term *con sordino*, but sometimes

composers use their native language. Mutes can be made out of any soft material—a knee-high nylon stocking works well for me.[13] When the mute is inserted, the lowest notes of the oboe (at least B♭ and B, depending on the placement of the mute) are blocked and will not speak. Muting may adversely affect intonation, especially in the low register.

Teeth on the Reed

Oboists most often place their teeth on the reed to produce extremely high notes (see chapter 2, "Upper-Register Fingerings"). For other notes, contact with teeth on the reed will produce a thin, edgy sound, and the pitch will rise. In addition, Nora Post recommends placing teeth on the upper blade of the reed to facilitate the execution of a rolling tone.[14]

Key Clicks

This technique, which works quite effectively on the flute, produces more disappointing results on the oboe. The inner chamber of the oboe does not resonate as well, and the sound—especially the change of pitch when different keys are struck—is barely audible. This can be remedied to some degree by amplification. Key clicks are somewhat more effective on the larger members of the oboe family, and they can be executed without the reed or bocal to increase resonance.

Noisy Inhalation

Professional oboists are trained to inhale silently, but it is very easy to make sounds while inhaling. Globokar's *Atemstudie* and David Rosenboom's *And Come Up Dripping* (CD track 37) both call for loud sucking sounds that are achieved by inhaling through the reed with slight lip pressure. In *Jo Ha Kyu*, Eleanor Hovda wanted a line with continuous and unbroken energy—and with articulated changes of gesture. She requested that the performer loudly inhale and exhale with the mouth off the reed. Indeed, she has even choreographed the breath, sometimes requesting several short exhalations before a big inhalation, for example. She uses graphic notation and verbal means to communicate this to the performer. The breath sounds are louder if the mouth is slightly closed and air is allowed to escape only through the front of the mouth.

Playing the Reed or Bocal Alone

Numerous composers and some improvisers have created interesting sounds with the reed alone, the bocal alone, or the reed and bocal sans instrument. Chenna and Salmi pointed out that it is possible to clasp the reed in a slightly open fist and to open and close your hand to make a "wah-wah" sound similar to a trumpet or trombone with a plunger.[15]

Playing without a Reed

Some creative performers have become absolute virtuosos at playing double-reed instruments without a reed. Joseph Celli wrote and performed the haunting *Sky: S for J* (for five English horns without reeds).[16] He has also perfected the techniques of performing *alla tromba* (using a trumpet-like embouchure) and blowing into the instrument more subtly to create whistle tones comparable to those made by a flute. Inhalation as well as exhalation can create interesting sounds.

Playing More than One Instrument Simultaneously

Anyone who has ever seen or heard a recording of Rahsaan Roland Kirk would have to be intrigued by this technique. The late and great Roland Kirk was a blind jazz musician who very convincingly performed two and sometimes three instruments simultaneously, often with intricate counterpoint and always with a lot of soul.[17] He sometimes played the English horn and tenor saxophone simultaneously. One of the challenges is simply how to hold more than one instrument at a time. A neck strap can help in this matter, but it's still pretty awkward. Another problem is how to play with only one hand. Obviously, the range will be limited. It's possible to tape some upper keys shut if lower notes are desired. Vinko Globokar called for this approach in *Dualité* for two oboes played by one oboist. The performer plays one oboe with his or her right hand while the left hand plays the other. Both oboes are in the mouth simultaneously. Globokar mentioned to me that the piece works best when the knees are also employed, raising and lowering the oboes to assist the embouchure. This approach certainly enhances the theatrical as well as the sonic gesture.

Rheita Technique

John Corigliano used this term to describe a technique in the last movement of his *Concerto for Oboe and Orchestra*. In the preface to the concerto, Corigliano mentions that the rheita is an Arabic oboe that is played with the entire reed inside the cavity of the mouth. He explained, "I had been to Marrakesh, where I heard the Arabic oboe accompanying cobras in the main square as they danced. These oboes are wooden and have a plastic disk around their top. The player puts the reed in his mouth, and presses his lips against the plastic disk, blowing his cheeks out, and you get that raucous, wonderful microtonal sound."[18] Rheita technique is achieved by placing the lips on the strings of the reed and blowing energetically.

A number of composers have requested a similar tone quality without using the term "rheita." George Crumb's *Ancient Voices of Children* includes a movement, "Dances of Ancient Earth," in which the oboe is requested to play with a "raw, primitive, shawm-like" tone and at a fortissimo dynamic (see figure 4-33). This technique is also effective on the oboe d'amore.

Figure 4-33   *Crumb, Dances of Ancient Earth from* Ancient Voices of Children

Marti Epstein included a section to be played "with a nasal tone like a Middle Eastern instrument" in *Thalia*, for oboe d'amore and live electronics. This technique is less effective on the English horn because of its darker tone quality.

Playing Non-Western Oboes

Many creative performers have studied and mastered non-Western double-reed instruments including the shenai, nadaswaram, or mukha veena from India or the p'iri from Korea, to name only a few. Almost every culture has its own oboe, and usually it's a raucous, Dionysian thing that makes our refined, polite oboe pale in comparison! A study of the recordings and the technique of various non-Western oboes can inspire performers and composers looking to broaden their musical horizons. A number of recordings of non-Western oboes are listed in the selected discography near the end of the book.

Notes

1. Iannis Xenakis, *Dmaathen* for oboe and percussion (Paris: Editions Salabert, 1976), measure 6.

2. Ursula Mamlock, *Five Capriccios* (New York: C. F. Peters Corp., 1968), Movement 1, measure 12–13.

3. Toru Takemitsu, *Distance pour hautbois avec ou sans sho* (Paris: Editions Salabert, 1972), measure 26–27 (page 2).

4. For a list of tremolos that includes quarter-tone combinations, see Peter Veale and Claus-Steffen Mahnkopf, *The Techniques of Oboe Playing* (Basel, Switzerland: Barenreiter Kassel, 1994).

5. Gardner Read, *Contemporary Instrumental Techniques* (New York: Schirmer Books, 1976), 136.

6. Heinz Holliger, *Pro Musica Nova* (Wiesbaden, Germany: Breitkopf & Hartel, 1972), appendix, 1.

7. Isang Yun, *Images* (Berlin: Bote & Bock, 1968), oboe part.

8. Bruno Bartolozzi, *New Sounds for Woodwind* (London: Oxford University Press, 1967), 22.

9. This description of smorzato is paraphrased from Phillip Rehfeldt's *New Directions for Clarinet*, rev. ed. (Berkeley: University of California Press, 1994), 63.

10. Heinz Holliger gives helpful suggestions for the performance of Globokar's vocalizations in Holliger, *Pro Musica Nova.*

11. Andrea Chenna with Massimiliano Salmi and Omar Zoboli, *Manuale Dell'Oboe Contemporaneo* [The Contemporary Oboe] (Milan: Rugginenti Editore, 1994), 59–60. Their explanation of the circular breathing technique is clear and detailed, and is highly recommended for further information on this subject.

12. From Berio, *Sequenza VII.*

13. Chenna and Salmi provide instructions for the construction of an oboe mute out of the core of a used Scotch Tape dispenser in *Manuale Dell'Oboe Contemporaneo*, 63.

14. Nora Post, "Monophonic Sound Resources for the Oboe," *Interface: Journal of New Music Research* 11 (1982): 150.

15. Chenna and Salmi, *Manuale Dell'Oboe Contemporaneo*, 61.

16. Included on *Organic Oboe* CD, OODisc#1.

17. A recommended recording is in the bibliography.

18. Interview, John Corigliano with Ev Grimes, 26 June 1987, New York City. Oral History, American Music archive, Yale University.

CHAPTER FIVE

Electronics for the Oboe: A Primer

Electronics are an integral part of the contemporary musician's world. Almost all active musicians find themselves in situations in which their instruments need to be amplified, many perform in radio broadcasts and create recordings, and some utilize electronics in order to expand their sound palette. This chapter will offer basic information and practical considerations regarding electronic applications for the oboe.

The diagram shown in figure 5-1 illustrates the standard configuration for any use of electronics.

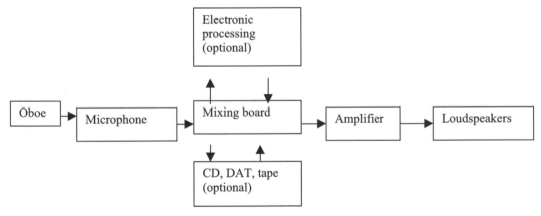

Figure 5-1   Electronics configuration

Amplification

In chamber music settings and particularly in solo performance, it is imperative that one has basic information about amplification. Consideration should be given to sound quality, ease of use, and elimination of problems such as excess key noise and feedback (the loud screech that occurs when the microphone picks up the signal from the loudspeaker). Various microphone setups are available: air microphones (the commonly used type that converts sound waves traveling through air into an audio signal), contact microphones (which are affixed to the reed or the instrument), and wireless microphones (an air microphone attached to the instrument that sends the signal to the mixer via radio waves). It has been my experience that there is no better tool to amplify the instrument and produce the truest and best sound quality than an air microphone. Contact microphones allow for freedom of movement and largely eliminate feedback. Unfortunately, they just don't yet sound as good as air microphones.

Sound emanates from the entire instrument, not just from the bell. For instance, if one plays an A 440, much of the sound will emanate from the G hole. Therefore, it is best to set the microphone somewhere along the middle of the instrument, about six to ten inches away. Another approach is to use two microphones, one for the top joint, and another for the bell. I always use two for the amplification of the English horn or oboe d'amore. For these larger instruments, place one microphone about six to ten inches from the middle of the top joint and the other the same distance from the top of the bell. Don't place the microphone directly under the bell, for this will result in overly loud and booming levels for the lowest notes on the instrument.

Once the microphone signal goes to the mixer, equalization (or EQ) is applied. This intensifies or attenuates various frequencies. For instance, it is possible to make a rich, dark oboe tone sound thin and bright by boosting the high frequencies and attenuating the lows. (Unfortunately, it's not so easy to make an unsubstantial tone sound good!) Performers need to understand EQ in order to ensure that the audience hears their desired tone quality.

We can learn something from popular music vocalists who are adroit at using the microphone. For instance, Frank Sinatra was known to use the microphone extraordinarily well to gain dynamic range with a naturally small voice. He could sing with an unforced, intimate tone and be heard above a loud band. It is crucial to understand that as soon as one steps in front of a microphone, one is playing an electronic instrument. The microphone is an extension of the instrument, and it must be used effectively. One needs to know where to stand, how to move, and the effects of various microphone placements. It requires practice, just like with any other instrumental technique.

Many performers are interested in exploring amplification and electronic effects, but they don't know where to start. I use an AKG C1000 S microphone for both amplification and recording. Also recommended is any microphone by Neumann. I would advise investing in the best microphone affordable. Next to the oboe and reed, it's the most critical part of the chain.

The standard sound system consists of several separate components: mixing board, electronic effects, amplifier, and loudspeakers. Simpler systems are available, for example the powered mixer, which combines the mixer, the amplifier, and optional effects; or self-powered speakers that usually include only the mixer and amplifier, and that take a signal directly from a microphone. Self-powered speakers are appropriate for situations in which only modest sound reinforcement is needed. The component system provides the greatest degree of flexibility and sonic sophistication. Following is basic information about the standard components in a sound system.

Mixing Board. Also known as a "mixer," this device combines and routes audio signals from a set of inputs to a set of outputs, usually with some adjustments to levels and EQ, often with electronic processing. A basic mixer usually has at least eight channels that receive signals from microphones, CD or tape, synthesizers, electronic effects, computer interface, or any combination of these. A professional mixing board might have as many as forty-eight or more channels. Signals come in at "line level" or the weaker "mic level." Most microphones need a pre-amplifier to boost the signal before it reaches the mixer. The pre-amp is usually included as part of the mixer, but it is also available as a separate unit.

Amplifiers. The main outputs of the mixer go to the power amplifier, and its function is to boost the signal. It will always be the last component before the loudspeakers in a sound system. The size and power of the amplifier must be appropriate to the loudspeakers and the room size in order to avoid distortion in loud passages or excess noise in soft passages.

Loudspeakers. A loudspeaker converts the electrical signal into sound. Often a loudspeaker will contain more than one driver in various shapes and sizes: small tweeters for high frequencies, large subwoofers for low frequencies, and separate drivers for mid-range frequencies. As with the amplifier, the loudspeaker needs to be appropriate to the room size and to the type of music being amplified. For example, a solo oboist would generally not need speakers with gigantic subwoofers. This type of speaker would be more suitable for a rock band with heavy bass frequencies.

Electronic Processing

Sophisticated electronic processing used to be available only to the privileged few who could gain access to major electronic music centers (usually at academic institutions). However, thanks to the invention of musical instrument digital interface (MIDI) and the booming popular music industry, electronic processing is now accessible and affordable to just about everyone. A variety of multi-effects processors, usually designed for guitarists and vocalists, are readily available on the market. There's not always a clear dividing line between electronic processing and amplification. For example, EQ is a type of processing, and in many instances, engineers will add some reverberation. Electronic effects can be used in a live performance, and this is referred to as "live electronics." In general, it is best to apply electronic effects after the audio signal has gone into the mixer. That way, you have control over the balance of processed versus acoustic sound. Note that depending on the size of the hall and the engineer's mix, the penetrating acoustic oboe sound is often audible and not totally colored by the live electronics. For recording purposes, it is customary to record the unprocessed sound and to apply effects afterwards. Following is a description of some of the most basic types of electronic processing.

Filters
Filters can be used to accentuate or attenuate certain frequencies within the full acoustic spectrum. A common type of filtering is EQ, discussed above, in which filters are applied to the amplified instrument's signal (with consideration to the electronic system and room) to sound as much as possible like the initial acoustic source. High-pass filters will not allow certain low frequencies through; low-pass filters will not allow certain high frequencies.

Wah-wah
The wah-wah effect is a simple type of filter system usually controlled by a foot pedal. It recreates the wah-wah sound made by a brass player using a plunger mute. As a player presses the foot pedal, it goes from attenuating the higher frequencies to attenuating the lower ones, creating a wah-wah effect. It is widely used by guitarists, but can be used by other instrumentalists as well. I had the honor of performing in the American premiere of Stockhausen's *Sternklang,*

Reverberating Eighth Note (courtesy T.J.)

a performance in which each of the instrumentalists used a custom-made filter pedal, similar to a wah-wah, in order to mimic vocal sounds.

Delay
Although the term "delay" is often used interchangeably with "echo," it has a broader meaning. If the audio signal is delayed in various ways, a number of effects will result. Reverberation is a type of delay that consists of multiple blended sound images (not individually discernable

"echoes") caused by reflection from walls, floor, ceiling, and other surfaces.[1] In contrast, echo refers to one or more distinct sound reiterations. Reverberation can be applied to a signal to mimic the acoustics of anything from a cathedral to a small room to a basketball arena. A reverb unit is often included in multi-effects processors. Delay can be created with digital or analog means. Some of us remember early delay systems created by tape loops: analog tape stretched between two machines. (It was always good sport to watch one part of the tape loop sag while the other tightened due to slight inequalities in speed of the two machines—and to wonder whether the tape would make it to the end of the piece!) Digital delay units are readily available and can create delays of a fraction of a second through several seconds after the original sound. Ingram Marshall's *Dark Waters* for English horn, tape, and digital delay uses a delay of eight seconds, and his *Holy Ghosts* for oboe d'amore and digital delay employs a much shorter delay that sometimes creates a canon to the eighth note.

Chorus, Phase, Flange

These are all effects achieved through manipulation of the delay process. In the chorus effect, several parallel delays are played, each with tiny variations in starting time (30–40 milliseconds). The effect, as the name implies, creates the impression of multiple sound sources, such as three oboes attempting to play in unison. In phasing and flanging, the original signal and the delay play back at slightly different speeds. The result gives the effect of a sweeping comb filter.

Pitch Shifter, Octave Divider, Harmonizer

These devices add one or more additional pitches to the original signal. A simple pitch shifter would always add the same interval, a major third, for instance. A "smart" harmonizer, a more sophisticated tool, would add intervals appropriate to a given scale. (For example, if shifting pitch up a third in a major scale, a harmonizer would add a major third to the tonic and a minor third to the super tonic.) An octave divider would add the upper or lower octave. Laurie Anderson has used pitch shifting extensively, and this effect can be heard in both the narration and the accompaniment of her well-known piece, "O Superman."

Envelope Modifier

An envelope is the shape of a sound, from attack through sustain to release. Envelopes can be modified, as in the bombastic attacks in the conclusion of Jack Vees's *Apocrypha* for oboe and tape (CD track 36). He used the ephemeral sound of an oboe reverberating in piano strings as the initial sound source, and gave it a sforzando brassy attack using a Buchla Spectral Processor.

Ring Modulation

A ring modulator combines two input signals. One signal is the carrier, and the other is the modulator. For example, if a voice is modified by a tremolo effect, the result would simply be a voice with varying amplitudes. (Tremolo effect changes amplitude or volume, while vibrato effect changes pitch.) If the tremolo goes faster than about twenty cycles per second, it would produce an audible pitch. A ring modulator would use this second signal to modulate the voice signal. The pitch of the carrier signal (the voice) would not change, but its timbre would be altered. This effect was used widely by the avant-garde electronic composers of the fifties and sixties, such as Karlheinz Stockhausen in *Mikrophonie II*. The effect was also used to create the robot voices in 1950s science fiction movies.

Vocoder

A vocoder takes an original signal (often a human voice) and splits it into a number of narrow frequency ranges. Each range is processed separately through an envelope follower and replaced with a synthesized sound, and is finally mixed as a single composite signal. The result is a synthesized sound that has many of the same properties as the initial sound source. The band Kraftwerk used this technique in "Expo 2000," as did Styx in their well-known "Mr. Roboto."

Distortion

This effect, popular among electric guitarists, distorts the tone. It is often available on multi-effects boxes, and can be applied to an oboe tone. In sections of Jack Vees's *Tattooed Barbie*, distortion is applied on both the oboe and the electric 12-string guitar (CD track 34).

Sampling

The sampler makes a digital picture of the original sound source and can play it back, like an instant recording. The sound can be processed and manipulated in any of the ways described above.

Noise Gate

A noise gate will turn off the audio signal passing through it when that signal falls below an adjustable threshold. This is a very handy tool for the oboist seeking to perform with live electronics while using an air microphone. The noise gate will help to eliminate feedback and to amplify and process only the oboe tone, not other sounds on stage.

Computer Interface

Through the language of MIDI, it is possible to interact with a computer with a sophistication and spontaneity comparable to that of chamber music. A pitch rider can follow the oboist's playing and initiate gestures when particular notes are played. In other pieces, a performer can set a tempo, and the computer can be programmed to follow. Todd Winkler's *Three Oboes* for oboe and live electronics features real-time harmonization, pitch shifting, delay, and other sound processing. Some composers have used MAX, a computer program that can sample the tone and transform it into another gesture or apply effects. The MAX program is used in Scott Lindroth's *Terza Rima* to play a synthesizer as well as to control digital effects. The effects device processes the live oboe sound as well as the synthesized timbres. This synthesized music comprises varied textural backgrounds for the oboe's melodic lines, and MAX can generate these textures indefinitely. The oboist (or an assistant) initiates each textural change with a foot pedal or some other MIDI input device.

Work with electronics can be very helpful to expand and inform any musician's ear training. Joseph Celli commented that electronics have had twofold use for him: "Live electronics in performance . . . [and] electronics informing me of what actually goes into producing sound."[2] He mentioned that electronics contributed to his understanding of overtone systems and the actual acoustic composition of a tone, and he noted that this perspective can instruct the way we play.

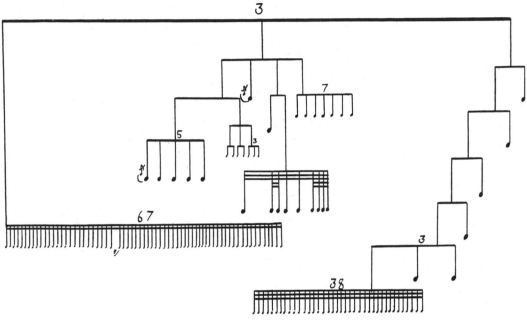

Complex Triplet (courtesy T.J.)

Recording

Oboe recordings tend to be of two types: a studio recording in a dry acoustical space, or a location recording in a space with acoustics suitable for the piece. In a studio recording, reverberation and EQ (and sometimes effects) are applied after the pure oboe sound is recorded. Microphone placement is usually up close. A location recording tends to emphasize the sound of the instrument's resonance in the acoustical space, and microphone placement tends to be slightly further away in order to capture some of the sound of the room. In either type of recording, a knowledgeable performer can usually be involved in decisions regarding microphone placement and equalization of the oboe tone. Recording engineers love to close-mike instruments—it gives them more control of the sound. However, the result is often strangely unlike the sound of an acoustic oboe—for example, the sound of the keys, saliva on the reed, and the breath are magnified out of proportion to an acoustic sound. Usually engineers will move the microphone back if the performer respectfully pleads with them, and usually the sound will be more attractive to the musician. Otherwise, the above discussion of microphone placement for amplification also applies to recordings.

Whenever possible, it is advisable to be involved in determining the specifics of EQ. Recording engineers respect musicians, and they usually want to help instrumentalists project their desired tone quality. The recording process offers a wonderful opportunity to explore the nuances of EQ. Listen to playbacks as often as possible, for they will teach you much. In most situations, it is best to put effects onto a separate track. That way, one can change them after the recording date, if desired. Once the recording is made, the editing process takes place. Today's digital editing makes it fairly simple to make minute and highly detailed changes. It is always a good idea to be involved in editing, if possible. Not only is it very helpful to understand the power and limits of the process, but it is also wonderful to have some influence as to which take is selected.

Notes

1. Gary Davis and Mark Jones, *Sound Reinforcement Handbook* (Milwaukee, Wisc.: Hal Leonard Publishing Co., 1987), part II, 5–17.

2. As quoted in Aaron Cohen, "Oboists and Electronics: Embracing a New Era," *International Double Reed Society Journal*, no. 25 (July 1997): 43.

Standard Fingering Chart for the Oboe

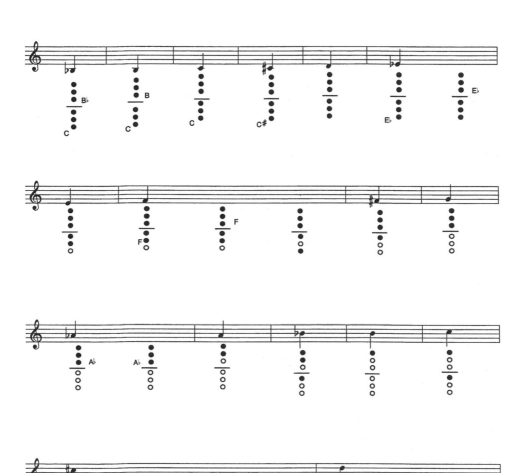

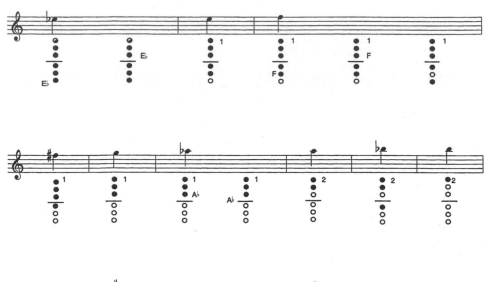

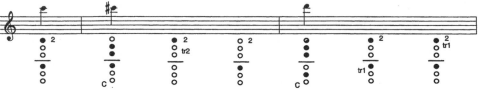

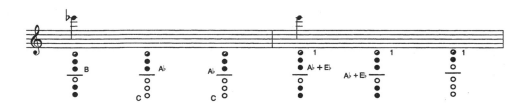

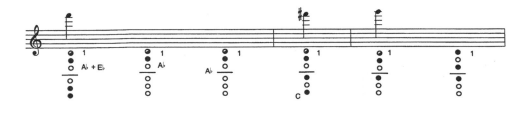

APPENDIX TWO

Apocrypha Score

The music reproduced in this appendix was commissioned by the Minnesota Composers Forum and appears with the following performance directions.

The lower staff of each system shows the major recognizable cues of the "tape" part. This part is now on an audio CD, available through Leisure Planet Music. The performer should synchronize with this by using a stopwatch or by following the timer on the CD player. Most of the interplay between the live player and prerecorded material are "soft" timing cues. However, the general tendency is that the live player leads the "tape" in the beginning of the piece and responds more to it at the end.

The two-channel playback of the tape part is best realized if the speakers are located front and rear of the performance space, as opposed to left and right. To be clear about which speaker is which, the front channel contains almost all of the sounds during the first minute of the piece. The performer should set up close to the front speaker so that the live and taped sounds are almost indistinguishable from one another. The performer may also use a microphone, not so much for volume but to enhance the blending with the other part. (If it is impossible to place speakers front and back, a left/right standard stereo system may be used with the performer standing far left on the stage.)

Much of the live part is about shading the main pitch given in the score by the use of alternate fingerings and trills. The fingerings shown in the score are suggestions that have proven to work well. Performers may substitute other alternate fingerings that achieve similar results.

The indication "ttr" indicates a timbral trill. This is achieved by trilling between the standard fingering and another that slightly alters the timbre or pitch.

The trill notation with two wavy lines (first appearing at 2:00) indicates a double trill. Trill using both the left and right hand fingerings or by using the first and second fingers of the right hand on the F♯ key and the screw just above it.

An asterisk placed above a note indicates that an alternate fingering should be used.

The indication "silently," which appears first at 7:00, is an indication for the player to "mime" that note or notes within the dotted lines. It is heard in the prerecorded part.

The numbers 1 or 2 appear in some fingerings. These indicate octave keys; 1 is the back octave key, and 2 is the side octave key.

APOCRYPHA

Jack Vees

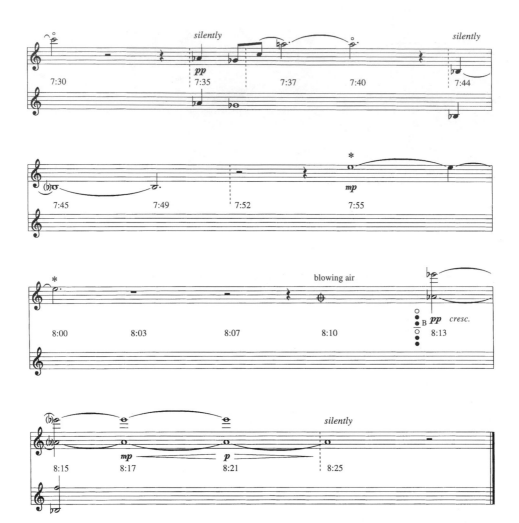

APPENDIX THREE

CD Contents

Techniques

1. Harmonics (:07)
2. Alternative Timbre Fingerings (:13)
3. Glissandi (:04)
4. Pitch Bends (:05)
5. Standard Multiphonics, 1–8 (:54)
6. Standard Multiphonics, 9–16 (:47)
7. Standard Multiphonics, 17–24 (:45)
8. Standard Multiphonics, 25–31 (:39)
9. Standard Multiphonics, 32–40 (:49)
10. Standard Multiphonics, 41–48 (:43)
11. Standard Multiphonics, 49–56 (:42)
12. Standard Multiphonics, 57–64 (:38)
13. Standard Multiphonics, 65–72 (:42)
14. Standard Multiphonics, 73–80 (:39)
15. Standard Multiphonics, 81–88 (:39)
16. Beating Multiphonics, 1–8 (:35)
17. Beating Multiphonics, 9–16 (:38)
18. Beating Multiphonics, 17–24 (:37)
19. Beating Multiphonics, 25–32 (:33)
20. Beating Multiphonics, 33–37 (:23)
21. Double Harmonics (#9) (:06)
22. Metamorphic Multiphonics, 1–5 (1:15)
23. Metamorphic Multiphonics, 6–11 (1:05)
24. Metamorphic Multiphonics, 12–18 (1:55)
25. Double Trill E-F (:06)
26. Microinterval Trill (:08)
27. Tremolos E-G (:07)
28. Double Tonguing, on air (:06)
29. Double Tonguing, with random pitches (:05)
30. Flutter Tonguing (:05)

31. Breath Accents (:06)
32. Rolling Tone (:08)

Excerpts of Repertoire

33. Scott Lindroth: *Terza Rima* for oboe and live electronics (:55)
34. Jack Vees: *Tattooed Barbie* for electrified oboe, 12-string electric guitar, and drum machine (1:12)
35. Eleanor Hovda: *Jo Ha Kyu* for oboe solo (:18)

Entire Compositions

36. Jack Vees: *Apocrypha* for oboe and tape (8:32)
37. David Rosenboom: *And Come Up Dripping* for oboe and live electronics (15:46)

Libby Van Cleve played oboe on all tracks. Jack Vees played guitar in *Tattooed Barbie*, and David Rosenboom performed on live electronics for *And Come Up Dripping*.

Tracks 1–35 and Track 36, *Apocrypha*, were recorded on October 5, 2002, at Yale University's Center for Studies in Music Technology, New Haven, Connecticut, David Budries, recording engineer. Track 37, *And Come Up Dripping*, resulted from a live performance on March 3, 2001, at the Engine 27 performance space in New York City, Jody Elff, recording engineer. The recording was later reprocessed and mastered by David Rosenboom in the composer's studio, California Institute of the Arts.

This CD was mastered by David Budries at Sound Situation Studios, Glastonbury, Connecticut.

About the Compositions

Apocrypha (1986) by Jack Vees

The oboe is the original sound source for all of the tape portions of Apocrypha. In fact, this piece was originally put together on old-fashioned analog tape, and it was the last time I did that. I recorded several samples of the oboe played into a piano, resonating the strings. This raw material was then processed through a Buchla 300, an early "digital" synthesizer and audio workstation, and mixed back onto a two-track tape. From its inception, the piece was designed for both the live and tape parts to be equal, not a solo voice with accompaniment. In the traditional sense, neither one carries the "theme." The real essence of the piece lies in the interdependence of each component, in the way they revolve about one another sometimes tightly, other times broadly, giving and receiving sonic material. (Quotation by Jack Vees)

And Come Up Dripping (1968) by David Rosenboom

"The sun- or sky-god descends to fructify the frozen earth in rain and lightning; there is a period of waiting; then the Young God is discovered in the first bloom of spring."

This recording of *And Come Up Dripping* by Libby Van Cleve and the composer is a new realization and updating of an original 1968 composition. The phrase, *And Come Up Dripping*, which I found in a book of colloquial sayings, is meant to evoke an image of new forms—new life forms or new musical forms—emerging from a primal soup of an underlying, self-organizing complexity created from the interaction of simple components. Thus, the form of each performance emerges every time anew. A fundamental process through which each form grows involves extension in time-space, realized by means of time delays that capture extended percepts in memory, which eventually coagulate into a mass, in this case, the mass of a musical architecture. Musical gestures notated with various graphical symbols provide initial genetic impulses of sound that become extended in this way. Complexity then arises from recombinant feedback in which every repeated phrase may be modified or mutated in three ways: 1) by processes which increase the information complexity of the oboe waveforms, making them less predictable, 2) by processes which decrease their information complexity, making them more predictable, and 3) by *gating*, a process imparting amplitude or loudness shapes to the musical gestures. The score provides a prototype scheme for all this, and the electronics performer is invited to use whatever means are at her or his disposal to make a faithful realization. In the first performances of *And Come Up Dripping*, the electronics part was realized with the aid of a homemade analog computer constructed by the composer. In this newly revived version, digital signal processing software was used to simulate the circuits used earlier. The oboist is free to choose the temporal ordering of the four main sections and where to begin on what is a kind of circular structure contained in each section. Some parts allow for considerable freedom in interpretation and some invite structured improvisation. The score was first published in *Source, Music of the Avant Garde* (Composer/Performer Edition, No. 6, 1969). (Quotation by David Rosenboom)

Selected Music Bibliography

The following compilation includes many major pieces in the oboe repertoire and a number of less well-known pieces. Manuscript compositions are noted as "manuscript," and addresses of composers have not been provided. Instead, readers are encouraged to consult such sources as the World Wide Web, *Dictionary of International Biography*, *Who's Who in Music*, ASCAP and BMI directories, and the *Directory of Music Faculties in Colleges and Universities*, *U.S. and Canada*.

Oboe Alone

Alexander, Kathryn. *Luminescence*. Manuscript, 1997.

Amy, Gilbert. *Jeux pour (1 à 4) hautbois*. London: Universal Edition, 1970.

Andriessen, Jurriaan. *Balocco*. Amsterdam: Donemus, 1960.

Andriessen, Louis. *A Flower Song II* for oboe solo. Amsterdam: Donemus, 1964.

———. *For Pauline O.* London: Boosey & Hawkes, 1995.

———. *vergeet mij niet* (for oboist who simultaneously plays piano). Manuscript, 1970.

Antoniou, Theodore. *Five Likes for Solo Oboe* (Oboe d'amore). Kassel, Germany: Bärenreiter, 1969.

Arnold, Malcolm. *Fantasy for Oboe*. London: Faber, 1966.

Baley, Virko. *Persona*. Troppo Note Publishing.

Bartolozzi, Bruno. *Collage*. Milan: Edizioni Suvini Zerboni, 1968.

Berio, Luciano. *Sequenza VII*. Vienna: Universal Edition, 1969.

———. *Sequenza VII*. Vienna: Universal Edition, 1969. Ed. Jacqueline Leclair, 1996.

Boone, Charles. *Springtime*. Paris: Éditions Salabert, 1980.

———. *Vermillion*. Paris: Éditions Salabert, 1970.

Bresnick, Martin. *Theme and Variations for Solo Oboe*. New Haven, Conn.: Common Muse Music Publishers, 1963.

Britten, Benjamin. *Six Metamorphoses After Ovid, Op. 49*. London: Boosey & Hawkes, 1951.

Cage, John. *4'33"*. New York: C.F. Peters Corp., 1952.

Cardew, Cornelius. *Volo Solo* for soloist or group of virtuosos. Manuscript, 1964.

Carter, Elliott. *A 6 Letter Letter* (1996). London: Boosey & Hawkes.

———. *Immer Neu*. London: Boosey & Hawkes, 1992.

———. *Inner Song* oboe solo from *Trilogy*. London: Hendon Music, 1992; distributed by Boosey & Hawkes.

Castiglioni, Niccoló. *Alef*. Mainz, Germany: Ars Viva Verlag, 1965.

———. *Gruezi*. Milan: Casa Ricordi, 1990.

Chavez, Carlos. *Upingos* (1957). New York: G. Schirmer, Inc., 1957.

Childs, Barney. *Five Little Soundpieces*. Tritone Press, 1959; distributed by Theodore Presser Co.

———. *Sonata*. New York: American Composers Alliance, 1958.

Clark, Mitchell. *A Little Suite of Geometrics*. Manuscript, 1976.

Cleary, David. *Bilbies VI* for any oboe. Manuscript, 1995.

Constantinides, Dinos. *Transformations for Oboe*. Greenleaf, Wisc.: Conners Publications, 1992.

Cope, David. *Indices*. Manuscript, 1971.

Corbett, Sidney. *Comino Incantations*. Manuscript, 1994.

Crawford-Seeger, Ruth. *Diaphonic Suite No. 1* (1930). New York: Continuo Music Press, Inc./Broude Brothers Limited, 1930.

Davies, Peter Maxwell. *First Grace of Light*. London: Boosey & Hawkes, 1991.

de Kruyf, Ton. *Echoi* canti e capricci per oboe solo, Op. 25. Berlin: Bote & Bock, 1969.

De Leeuw, Ton. *Music for Oboe*. Amsterdam: Donemus, 1969.

Denisov, Edison. *Solo für Oboe*. Wiesbaden, Germany: Breitkopf & Härtel, 1971.

Donatoni, Franco. *Incisi*. Milan: Casa Ricordi, 1995.

Dorati, Antal. *Cinq Pièces pour le Hautbois*. London: Boosey & Hawkes, 1981.

Fine, Vivian. *Second Solo*. New York: American Composers Alliance, 1957.

Finnissy, Michael. *Moon's Goin' Down*. Karlsruhe, Germany: Edition Modern, 1980.

Fulkerson, Jim. *Patterns VII*. Karlsruhe, Germany: Edition Modern, 1975.

Globokar, Vinko. *Atemstudie*. New York: C.F. Peters Corp., 1971.

———. *Dualité* (for two oboes played by one oboist). Peters.

Goldberg, William. *Urns*. Manuscript, 1982.

Goldstein, Malcolm. *A Summoning of Focus*. Manuscript, 1977.

Gordon, Morgan. *The Wisdom of Cats*. Manuscript, 1998.

Gryc, Stephen. *Three Excursions*. Manuscript, 1991.

Harbison, John. *Amazing Grace*. New York: G. Schirmer, Inc., 1972.

Holliger, Heinz. *Sonata*. Mainz, Germany: Schott Musik International, 1956–1957, rev. 1999.

———. *Studie über Mehrklnge* Wiesbaden, Germany: Breitkopf & Härtel, 1971.

———. *Studie II*. Mainz, Germany: Ars Viva Verlag, 1981.

Hovda, Eleanor. *Jo Ha Kyu*. Manuscript, 1990.

Huber, Nicolaus. *Vor und zurück*. Wiesbaden, Germany: Breitkopf & Härtel, 1981.

Hübler, Klaus. *Grave e sfrenato*. Wiesbaden, Germany: Breitkopf & Härtel, 1985.

Ichiyanagi, Toshi. *Cloud Figures*. Tokyo: Schott Japan, 1984.

Jarvinen, Arthur. *The Fifteen Fingers of Dr. Wu*. Los Angeles: Leisure Planet Music, 1987.

Johnson, Tom. *Infinite Melodies*. Paris: Editions 75, 1986.

———. *Rational Melodies*. Paris: Editions 75, 1982.

Kagel, Mauricio. *Atem: für einen Bläser (for one wind player)*. London: Universal Edition, 1970.

Kalogeras, Alexandros. *Nomos*. Manuscript, 1990.

Krenek, Ernst. *Sonatina*. New York: Broude Brothers, 1956.

Lamb, John David. *Pasatiempos*. Seattle, Wash.: Näckens Vänner, 1993.

Lebenbom, Elaine. *Sonnets for a Solitary Oboe*. Manuscript, 1982.

Leehmann, Hans Ulrich. *Monodie*. Mainz, Germany: Schott, 1970.

LeFanu, Nicola. *Soliloquy*. London: Chester Music and Novello & Co., 1966.

Levin, Todd. *Asides on the Oboe (. . . after Couperin)*. Manuscript, 1983–1984.

Lewis, Robert Hall. *Monophony II*. Vienna: Doblinger, 1973.

Lindroth, Scott. *Whistle Stop*. St. Paul, Minn.: Davidge Publishing, 1990.

Lüttmann, Reinhard. *Méditation I—Fantasie für un Thème de Plain-Chant Chorlbearbeitung*. Paris: Alphonse Leduc, 1973.

Mabry, Drake. *Lament for Astralabe*. Milan: Rugginenti Editore, 1980.

———. *Three Preludes*. San Diego: Drake Mabry Publishing, 1995.

Machajdík, Peter. *Kirin*. Edition Hudba 019, 2000.

Maderna, Bruno. *Solo* for oboe (or musette, oboe d'amore, or English horn) Milan: Casa Ricordi, 1971.

Mahnkopf, Claus-Steffen. *Gorgoneion für Oboe*. Kassel, Germany: Bärenreiter, 1990.

Mahoney, Shafer. *Everything Has A Clock*. Manuscript, 1994.

Méfano, Paul. *Asahi*. Paris: Éditions Musicales Européennes, 1992.

Mellits, Marc. *Parking Violation*. Manuscript, 1999.

Morehead, Patricia. *Design One*.

Morricone, Ennio. *Gabriel's Oboe*.

Parik, Ivan. *Sonata for Oboe*. Slovakia: Music Information Centre, 1973.

Perry, Jeffrey. *Minty Squid*. Baton Rouge, La.: What's That Noise Music, 1985.

Persichetti, Vincent. *Parable III*. Bryn Mawr, Pa.: Elkan-Vogel, Inc., 1968.

Peterson, Geoffrey. *Sonata for Solo Oboe*. Bryn Mawr, Pa.: Theodore Presser Co., 1996.

Pinkham, Daniel. *Reeds*. New York: C.F. Peters Corp., 1987.

Polin, Claire. *Telemannicon*. New York: Seesaw Music Corp., 1974.

Possio, Gianni. *Et . . . le temps s'arrete*. Milan: Rugginenti Editore, 1986.

Pousseur, Henri. *Caracteres Madrigalesques*. Manuscript, 1965.

———. *Flexions III*. Manuscript, 1979.

Rands, Berhard. *Memo 8*. Miami, Fla.: Helicon Music Corp., 2001; distributed by European American Music Distributors.

Reinhard, Johnny. *Melanin*. Manuscript, 1997.

Roseman, Ronald. *Partita for Solo Oboe*. Richmond, Va.: International Opus, 1997.

Schat, Peter. *Thema, Op. 21*. Amsterdam: Donemus, 1970.

Shatin, Judith. *Assembly Line #1*. Wendigo Music, 1983; distributed by Norruth Music.

Shinohara, Makoto. *Réflexion*. Wiesbaden, Germany: Breitkopf & Härtel, 1970.

Silverman, Faye-Ellen. *Oboe-sthenics*. New York: Seesaw Music Corp., 1980.

Singer, Lawrence. *Work*. Milan: Edizioni Suvini Zerboni, 1968.

Smith, Stuart. *Hawk*. Akron, Ohio: Sonic Art Editions, 1991.

Steinke, Greg. *Four Desultory Episodes*. New York: Seesaw Music Corp., 1975.

Stockhausen, Karlheinz. *In Freundscaft* (version for oboe solo). Kürten, Germany: Stockhausen-Verlag, 1979.

———. *Plus Minus*. London: Universal Edition, 1965, rev. 1974.

———. *Spiral* for a soloist (1968). London: Universal Edition, 1968.

Swartz, Dr. Keith D. *O, Boe!* Manuscript, 1998.

Takemitsu, Toru. *Distance pour hautbois avec ou sans sho*. Paris: Éditions Salabert, 1972.

Tisné, Antonie. *Dinos I and II*. Paris: Edition Transatlantiques, 1973.

Tomasi, Henri. *Evocations*. Paris: Alphonse Leduc, 1969.

Usher, Julia. *A Reed in the Wind*. London: Primavera, 1981.

Vees, Jack. *Instrumentalation No. 1*. Los Angeles: Leisure Planet Music, 1984.

Wildberger, Jacques. *Rondeau*. Karlsruhe, Germany: Edition Modern, 1960.

Wolff, Christian. *Isn't This a Time?* New York: C.F. Peters Corp., 1982.

Wyttenback, Jürg. *Sonata for Oboe Solo*. Wiesbaden, Germany: Breitkopf & Härtel, 1962, rev. 1972.

Yun, Isang. *Piri*. Berlin: Bote & Bock, 1971.

Zannoni, Davide. *Malcomino*. Manuscript, 1996.

English Horn Alone

Andriessen, Jurriaan. *Elegia*. Amsterdam: Donemus, 1967.

Bernstein, Charles Harold. *Reverie and Eglise*. Culver City, Calif.: Siempre Musica, 1996.

Caltabiano, Ronald. *Sonata* for solo English horn or oboe. Bryn Mawr, Pa.: Merion Music, Inc., 1986, rev. 1998; distributed by Theodore Presser Co.

Childs, Barney. *Four Involutions*. Tritone Press, 1955; distributed by Theodore Presser Co.

Clark, Mitchell. *Elegy*. Manuscript, 1973.

———. *Landscape*. Manuscript, 1980.

Felciano, Richard. *Dark Landscape*. Manuscript, 1985.

Johnson, Tom. *Infinite Melodies*. Paris: Editions 75, 1986.

———. *Rational Melodies*. Paris: Editions 75, 1982.

Maderna, Bruno. *Solo* for oboe (or musette, oboe d'amore, or English horn). Milan: Casa Ricordi, 1971.

Mitchell, Darleen. *Dichotic Sounds 4*. New York: American Composers Editions, 1987.

Persichetti, Vincent. *Parable*. Bryn Mawr, Pa.: Elkan-Vogel, Inc., 1975.

Singer, Lawrence. *Senzione*. Manuscript, 1981.

Tisné, Antonie. *Dinos III* Paris: Edition Transatlantiques, 1973.

Tomasi, Henri. *Evocations*. Paris: Alphonse Leduc, 1969.

Oboe and Piano or Keyboard

Adams, Daniel. *Augustine Shadows*. Manuscript, 1996.

Andriessen, Hendrik. *Ballade*. Amsterdam: Donemus, 1952.

Appledorn, Mary Jeanne van. *Incantations for Oboe and Piano*. Edited by Anderson. Arsis Press, 1998; distributed by Empire Publishing Services, Studio City, Calif.

Badings, Henk. *Canzona* for oboe and organ. Amsterdam: Donemus, 1938.

———. *Cavatina*. Amsterdam: Donemus, 1952.

Bahr, Jason. *Lacerations*. Manuscript, 1997.

Bainbridge, Simon. *Music for Mel and Nora*. London: United Music Publishers Ltd., 1979.

Barber, Samuel. *Canzonetta*. New York: G. Schirmer, Inc., 1978.

Bassett, Leslie. *Dialogues for Oboe and Piano*. New York: C.F. Peters Corp., 1987.

Bennett, Richard Rodney. *After Syrinx I*. London: Chester Music and Novello & Co., 1982.

Birtwistle, Harrison. *An Interrupted Endless Melody*. London: Boosey & Hawkes, 1996.

Bolcom, William. *For the Continuation of Life: Aubade*. Bryn Mawr, Pa.: Theodore Presser Co., 1982.

Boulanger, Lili. *Piece*. 1914, possibly lost or destroyed.

Britten, Benjamin. *Temporal Variations*. London: Faber Music, 1936.

———. *Two Insect Pieces*. London: Faber Music, 1935.

Castiglioni, Niccoló. *Rima*. Manuscript, 1984.

Cowell, Henry. *Three Ostinati*. Bryn Mawr, Pa.: Theodore Presser Co., 1937.

Crumb, George. *Three Pastoral Pieces*. New York: C.F. Peters Corp., 1959.

Dutilleux, Henri. *Sonate*. Paris: Alphonse Leduc, 1947.

Eder, Helmut. *Tre Pezzi Espressivi*, Op. 37. Kassel, Germany: Bärenreiter, 1963.

Erber, James. *Seguente*. London: G. Ricordi & Co., 1980.

Ferneyhough, Brian. *Coloratura*. New York: C.F. Peters Corp., 1966.

Fontyn, Jacqueline. *Compagnon de la Nuit*. POM, Leuven, Belgium, 1989; distributed by Peermusic Classical.

Holliger, Heinz. *Sonata*. Mainz, Germany: Schott Musik International, 1957, rev. 1999.

Hovhaness, Alan. *Sonata* for Hichiriki (oboe) and Sho (organ). New York: C.F. Peters Corp., 1962.

Huber, Klaus. *Noctes* for oboe and harpsichord. Mainz, Germany: Schott Musik International, 1961.

Jolivet, Andre. *Chant pour les piroguiers de l'Orenoque*. London: Boosey & Hawkes, 1953.

———. *Serenade* for oboe and piano. Billaudot, 1945; distributed by Boosey & Hawkes.

Julstrom, Clifford A. *Puck after "Midsummer Night's Dream."* Macomb, Ill.: Julstrom Enterprises, 1980.

Kaminsky, Laura. *Interpolations on Utopia Parkway*. Manuscript, 1994, rev. 1997.

Kirby, Paul. *Three Short Pieces*. Manuscript, 1978.

Kondoh, Harue. *Poema*. Tokyo: The Japan Federation of Composers, 1989.

Krenek, Ernst. *Vier Stücke* (Four Pieces). Kassel, Germany: Bärenreiter, 1966.

Kupferman, Meyer. *New Serenades '89*. Rhinebeck, N.Y.: Soundspells Productions, 1989.

Larson, Libby. *Kathleen, as she was*. New York: G. Schirmer, Inc., 1989.

Lehmann, Hans Ulrich. *Rota* for oboe and harpsichord. Wiesbaden, Germany: Breitkopf & Härtel, 1974.

Lifchitz, Max. *Night Voices No. 3*. Manuscript, 1984.

Luening, Otto. *Notti nel Giardino di Chopin (Night in the Garden of Chopin: Nocturne for Oboe and Piano)*. Manuscript, 1958.

Lutoslawski, Witold. *Epitaph*. London: Chester Music and Novello & Co., 1979.

MacDowell, Edward, arranged Smit. *Three Pieces by Edward MacDowell*. Bryn Mawr, Pa.: Theodore Presser Co.

Mamlok, Ursula. *Five Capriccios*. New York: C.F. Peters Corp., 1968.

Norden, Maarten van. *Lonesome Hobo*. Amsterdam: Donemus, 1992.

Pinkham, Daniel. *Variations* for oboe and organ. New York: C.F. Peters Corp., 1970.

Pisk, Paul. *Suite*. Montevideo, Uruguay: Instituto Interamericano de Musicología, 1947; distributed by Southern Music Co., New York.

Piston, Walter. *Suite for Oboe and Piano*. Boston: E.C. Schirmer, 1931.

Rathburn, Jeffrey. *Threnody*. West Linn, Oreg.: Amoris International, 1991.

Rochberg, George. *La Bocca Della Verita*. Impero, 1960; distributed by Theodore Presser Co.

Rorem, Ned. *An Oboe Book*. London: Boosey & Hawkes, 1999.

Rota, Nino. *Elegia*. Paris: Alphonse Leduc, 1954.

Roxburgh, Edwin. *Antares*. London: United Music Publishers Ltd., 1988.

———. *Images*. London: United Music Publishers Ltd., 1967.

Salonen, Esa-Pekka. *Second Meeting*. London: Chester Music and Novello & Co., 1992.

Salzedo, Leonard. *Cantiga Mozárabe*. West Linn, Oreg.: Amoris International, 1970.

Schickele, Peter. *Gardens*. New York: Tetra Music, 1975; distributed by A. Broude.

Schuller, Gunther. *Sonata for Oboe and Piano*. New York: McGinnis & Marx, 1958.

Schwartz, Elliott. *Second Thoughts*. New York: American Composers Alliance, 1984.

Shapey, Ralph. *Rhapsodie*. Bryn Mawr, Pa.: Theodore Presser Co, 1957.

———. *Sonate*. Bryn Mawr, Pa.: Theodore Presser Co., 1952.

Shinohara, Makoto. *Obsession*. Paris: Alphonse Leduc, 1960.

Tower, Joan. *Opa Eboni*. New York: American Composers Alliance, 1967.

———. *Toccanta* for oboe and harpsichord. New York: G. Schirmer, Inc., 1997.

Ussachevsky, Vladimir. *Triskelion*. New York: C.F. Peters Corp., 1988.

Voormolen, Alexander. *Pastorale*. Amsterdam: Donemus, 1940.

Wilder, Alec. *Sonata*. Wilder Music, 1969. Sole selling agent S. Fox, New York.

Wilson, Richard. *Character Studies*. New York: Peermusic Classical, 1982.

Wolpe, Stefan. *Sonate*. New York: McGinnis & Marx, 1938.

Wuorinen, Charles. *Composition for Oboe and Piano*. New York: C.F. Peters Corp., 1972.

Zaimont, Judith. *Doubles*. Blaine, Minn.: Jeanné, Inc., 1993.

Zeljenka, Ilja. *Mobilia*. Slovakia: Music Information Centre, 1994.

Zonn, Paul. *Chroma*. New York: American Composers Alliance, 1968.

English Horn and Piano or Keyboard

Andriessen, Hendrik. *Variations on a theme of F. J. Haydn*. Amsterdam: Donemus. 1968.

Bainbridge, Simon. *Mobile*. London: United Music Publishers Ltd., 1991.

Carter, Elliott. *Pastoral*. Bryn Mawr, Pa.: Merion Music, 1940; distributed by Theodore Presser Co.

Luening, Otto. *Variations on a Theme-song for a Silent Movie*. Manuscript, 1937.

Read, Gardner. *Poem II* for English horn and organ. Champaign, Ill.: Media Press, Inc., 1996.

Oboe and Electronics

Bennett, Myron. *Dialogue for One* for oboe doubling English horn and two tape recorders. Manuscript, 1969.

Bimstein, Phillip. *Half Moon at Checkerboard Mesa* for oboe and tape. Springdale, Utah: Franklin Stark Music, 1997.

Brunner, George. *Teaching No Talking* for oboe and tape. Manuscript.

Cage, John. *Fontana Mix* for any instrument or combination of instruments. New York: C.F. Peters Corp., 1958.

Carl, Robert. *Yearning* for oboe with digital delay, processing and tape. Manuscript, 1997.

Eisma, Will. *Adela I* for oboe and tape. Amsterdam: Donemus, 1977.

Erickson, Robert. *Nine and A Half for Henry (and Wilbur and Orville)* for instruments and tape. New York: Seesaw Music Corp., 1970.

Hatzis, Christos. *Byzantium* for oboe and tape. Manuscript, 1991.

Hays, Sorrel. *Take Back a Country Road*. New York: Tallapoosa Music, 1992.

———. *The Clearing Way* from *Sound Shadows*. New York: Tallapoosa Music, 1990.

Heussenstamm, George. *Alchemy, Op. 60* for oboe with tape. Manuscript, 1976. (Note: This won the 1977 composition competition of the International Double Reed Society.)

Holliger, Heinz. *Cardiophonie für oboe und 3 Magnetophone*. Mainz, Germany: Schott Musik International, 1971.

Jaffe, David A. *Impossible Animals* for oboe and tape. Manuscript, 1990.

Johnston, Ben. *Casta* for any solo instrument with tape loop. Champaign, Ill.: Media Press, Inc., 1970.

Justel, Elsa. *Feuillage de Silence* for flute, oboe, and tape. Manuscript, 1994.

Krenek, Ernst. *Aulokithara* for oboe, harp and tape. Vienna: Doblinger, 1972.

LaBarbara, Joan. *L'albero dalle foglie azzurre* for oboe and tape. Joan LaBarbara Music, 1989.

Leach, Mary Jane. *Xantippe's Rebuke* for oboe and tape. New York: Ariadne Music, 1993.

Lindroth, Scott. *Terza Rima* for oboe and live electronics. St. Paul, Minn.: Davidge Publishing, 1995.

Louvier, Alain, ed. *Mélanges Volume 2—oeuvres faciles pour flute (ou hautbois) et bande magnétique* (1984). Paris: Heugel et cie., Alphonse Leduc, 1984. (Contains works by Bousch, Louvier, Schwarz, Savouret, and Risset.)

Nazor, Craig. *Inverted Canons* for oboe and tape. Manuscript.

Phillips, Mark. *Sonic Landscapes* for oboe and tape. Manuscript, 1989.

Reynolds, Roger. *Islands from Archipelago: I. Summer Island* for oboe and computer-generated tape. New York: C.F. Peters Corp., 1984.

Rosenboom, David. *And Come Up Dripping* for oboe with live electronic processing. Santa Clarita, Calif.: David Rosenboom Publishing, 1968.

Roxburgh, Edwin. *Elegy* for oboe, electronics, and chamber ensemble. London: United Music Publishers Ltd., 1981.

Schwartz, Elliott. *Extended Oboe* for oboe and tape. New York: American Composers Alliance, 1972.

Stockhausen, Karlheinz. *Solo* for a melody instrument with feedback. Vienna: Universal Edition, 1966.

Szeghy, Iris. *In Between* for oboe and tape. Slovakia: Music Information Centre, 1993.

Ussachevsky, Vladimir. *Pentagram* for oboe and tape. Manuscript, 1980.

Vees, Jack. *Apocrypha* for oboe and tape. Los Angeles: Leisure Planet Music, 1986.

———. *Tattooed Barbie* for oboe with live electronics, electric 12-string guitar, and computer drums. Los Angeles: Leisure Planet Music, 1992.

Winkler, Todd. *Three Oboes* for oboe and electronics. Providence, R.I.: Todd Winkler Music, 1989.

English Horn and Electronics

Chadabe, Joel. *Street Scene* for English horn, tape, and projections. New York: Carl Fischer, 1967.

Hellerman, William. *One into Another (Ariel)*. New York: American Composers Alliance, 1972.

Marshall, Ingram. *Dark Waters* for English horn with live electronics and tape. Hamden, Conn.: IBU Music, 1995.

Misurell-Mitchell. *Deconstruction Blues* for English horn and DX7. Manuscript.

Sekon, Joe. *The Fester Merchant*. Manuscript, 1973.

Silverman, Faye-Ellen. *Layered Lament*. New York: Seesaw Music Corp, 1983.

Multiple Oboes or English Horns

Amy, Gilbert. *Jeux pour (1 à 4) hautbois*. London: Universal Edition, 1970.

Andriessen, Jurrian. *Divertimento* for two oboes and English horn. Amsterdam: Donemus, 1989.

Ardévol, José. *Sonata a Tres No. 4* for two oboes and English horn. New York: Southern Music Publishing Co., 1945.

Badings, Henk. *Trio no. 4A* for two oboes and English horn. Amsterdam: Donemus, 1946.

Carr, Edwin. *Waiheke Island* for oboe, oboe d'amore (opt. oboe), English horn, and bass oboe (opt. bassoon). West Linn, Oreg.: Amoris International, 1997.

Childs, Barney. *Changes* for three oboes. New York: American Composers Alliance, 1959.

———. *Take 5* for any five instruments. Tritone Press, 1962; distributed by Theodore Presser Co.

Clark, Mitchell. *Neglected Topiary in Lingering Afternoon Sunlight* for two English horns. Manuscript, 1997.

Globokar, Vinko. *Discours III* for five oboes. Frankfurt: Henry Litolff's Verlag/C.F. Peters Musikverlag, 1969.

Hovda, Eleanor. *MultiCelli*. Manuscript.

Jarvinen, Arthur. *A Conspiracy of Crows* for three oboes, or any combination of oboe, oboe d'amore, English horn, and bass oboe. Los Angeles: Leisure Planet Music, 2000.

Lomon, Ruth. *Furies* for pre-recorded oboes (oboe, oboe d'amore and English horn) and oboe. Manuscript.

Mabry, Drake. *Prelude Trio* for three oboes. San Diego: Drake Mabry Publishing, 1995.

Macbride, David. *Rozmarin* for English horn quartet and offstage oboe. Manuscript, 1996.

Machajdík, Peter. *Solitude* for four oboes. Bratislava, Slovakia: Music Information Centre of the Music Fund, 1999.

Matsudaira, Yoritsune. *6 Modes pour 2 Hautbois*. Manuscript.

Read, Gardner. *Phantasmagoria* for English Horn, Oboe, Oboe d'Amore and Organ. Champaign, Ill.: Media Press, Inc., 1988.

Roseman, Ronald. *Sonata for Two Oboes and Harpsichord*. New York: American Composers Alliance, 1977.

———. *Trio for Two Oboes and English Horn*. New York: American Composers Alliance, 1960.

Roxburgh, Edwin. *Shadow-Play* for two oboes and English horn. London: United Music Publishers Ltd., 1984.

Salzedo, Leonard. *Bailables* for oboe, oboe d'amore (opt. oboe), English horn, and bass oboe (opt. bassoon). West Linn, Oreg.: Amoris International.

Sixta, Jozef. *Trio* for two oboes and English horn. Slovakia: Music Information Centre.

Sollberger, Harvey. *Two Oboes* for two oboes. New York: McGinnis & Marx, 1963.

Stevens, Thomas. *Triangles IV* for English horn with three live or pre-recorded oboes. Bulle, Switzerland: Editions BIM, 1994.

Takahashi, Yuji. *Operation Euler* for 2 or 3 oboes. New York: C.F. Peters Corp., 1969.

Urbaitis, Mindaugas. *Inventions* for 3–5 oboes. Vilnius, Lithuania: "Vaga" Publishers, Ltd., 1976.

Whittenburg, Charles. *Jambi* for two oboes. New York: McGinnis & Marx, 1968.

Wilder, Alec. *Suite* for oboe and English horn. Newton Centre, Mass.: Margun Music, 1981.

Wozniak, Chad. *Oboe Consort in b Minor* for 2 oboes, oboe d'amore, English horn, and heckelphone. Manuscript, 1976.

Wuorinen, Charles. *Bicinium* for 2 oboes. New York: C.F. Peters Corp., 1966.

Yun, Isang. *Inventionen* for two oboes. Berlin: Bote & Bock, 1983.

Oboe with Miscellaneous Larger Ensembles

Alexander, Joe. *Wechselnd Farben* for oboe and multipercussion. Manuscript, 1986.

Andriessen, Hendrik. *Concertino* for oboe and strings. Amsterdam: Donemus, 1970.

Andriessen, Louis. *Anachronie II* for oboe and chamber ensemble. Amsterdam: Donemus, 1969.

Bainbridge, Simon. *Concertante in Moto Perpetuo* for oboe and ensemble. London: United Music Publishers Ltd., 1983.

Baley, Virko. *Orpheus Singing* for oboe and string quartet. Troppo Note Publishing, 1995.

Bartolozzi, Bruno. *Concertazioni* for oboe and ensemble. Milan: Edizioni Suvini Zerboni, 1966.

Bennett, Richard Rodney. *Concerto* for oboe and strings. London: Universal Edition, 1970.

Benguerel, Xavier. *Music for Oboe and Chamber Ensemble*. Celle, Germany: Moeck Verlag, 1969.

Berger, Arthur. *Duo* for oboe and clarinet. New York, C.F. Peters Corp., 1952.

Berio, Luciano. *Chemins IV* for oboe and eleven strings. Milan: Universal Edition, 1975.

Biriotti, Leon. *Jerusalem Symphony* for oboe, soprano, and strings. Manuscript.

Birtwistle, Harrison. *Pulse Sampler* for oboe and claves. London: Univeral Edition, 1981.

Bolcom, William. *A Spring Concertino for Oboe and Small Orchestra*. Bryn Mawr, Pa.: Theodore Presser Co., 1987.

Bolle, James. *Oboe Concerto*. New York: Peermusic Classical, 1992.

Bozza, Eugène. *Contrastes II* for oboe and bassoon. Paris: Alphonse Leduc, 1977.

Britten, Benjamin. *Phantasy Quartet*. London: Boosey & Hawkes, 1932.

Cage, John. *Music for Wind Instruments*. New York: Henmar Press, Inc., 1961.

———. *Ryoanji for oboe solo with percussion or orchestral obbligato and ad libitum with other pieces of the same title*. New York: Henmar Press, Inc., 1983.

Cardew, Cornelius. *Volo Solo* for soloist or group of virtuosos. Manuscript, 1964.

Carter, Elliott. *Concerto* for oboe and orchestra. London: Boosey & Hawkes, 1986–1987.

———. *Oboe Quartet*. London: Boosey & Hawkes, 2001.

———. *Quintet* for piano and winds. London: Boosey & Hawkes, 1991.

———. *Sonata* for oboe, flute, cello, and harpsichord. New York: Associated Music Publishers, Inc., 1952.

———. *Trilogy* for harp and oboe. London: Boosey & Hawkes, 1992.

Chihara, Paul. *Ceremony* for oboe, two violoncelli, double bass, and percussion. New York: C.F. Peters Corp., 1971.

Cobo, Luis Andrei. *Prelude and Millennium* for oboe and string quartet. Manuscript, 1997.

Coleman, Ornette. *In Honor of NASA and Its Planetary Soloists* for string quartet, oboe/English horn/mukha veena. Manuscript.

Corigliano, John. *Aria* for oboe and five strings. New York: G. Schirmer, Inc., 1985.

———. *Oboe Concerto*. New York: G. Schirmer, Inc., 1975.

Cowell, Henry. *Hymn and Fuguing Tune No. 10* for oboe and strings. Manuscript, 1955.

Crawford Seeger, Ruth. *Three Songs* (on poems by Carl Sandburg) for alto, oboe, piano, percussion, and optional chamber orchestra. San Francisco: New Music Edition, 1930–1932.

Crockett, Donald. *Celestial Mechanics* for oboe and string quartet. St. Louis, Mo.: MMB Music, Inc., 1990.

Crumb, George. *Ancient Voices of Children* for oboe in a chamber ensemble with mezzo soprano, boy soprano, mandolin, harp, electric piano, and percussion. New York: C.F. Peters Corp., 1970.

Daugherty, Michael. *Firecracker* for oboe and chamber ensemble. New York: Peermusic Classical, 1991.

Davidovsky, Mario. *Quartetto no. 2* for oboe and strings. New York: C.F. Peters, 1997.

———. *Synchronisms No. 8* for woodwind quintet and tape. Manuscript, 1974.

Davies, Peter Maxwell. *Strathclyde Concerto No. 1* for oboe and orchestra. London: Boosey & Hawkes, 1987.

Deak, Jon. *The Bremen Town Musicians* for woodwind quintet. New York: Carl Fischer, 1990.

———. *Vasilisa, or, A Young Girl Meets Baba-Yaga* for woodwind quintet. Manuscript, 1994.

de Kruyf, Ton. *Mosaic* for oboe and string trio. Berlin: Bote & Bock, 1969.

Denisov, Edison. *Concerto* for flute, oboe, piano, and percussion. Vienna: Universal Edition, 1986.

———. *Konzert* for oboe and orchestra. Hamburg: Hans Sikorski, 1992.

———. *Romantisches Musik* for oboe, violin, viola, cello and harp. London: Universal Edition, 1968.

———. *Trio* for oboe, cello and harpsichord (1981). Leipzig, Germany: C.F. Peters, 1981.

Dlugoszewski, Lucia. *Amor Elusive Empty August* for woodwind quintet. Newton Center, Mass.: Margun, 1979.

Dobrowolski, Andrzej. *Musik für Orchester und Oboe solo*. Celle, Germany: Editions Moeck, 1985.

Donatoni, Franco. *Blow* for woodwind quintet. Milan: Casa Ricordi, 1989.

———. *Espressivo* for oboe and orchestra. Milan: Edizioni Suvini Zerboni, 1972.

———. *Triplum* for flute, oboe, and clarinet. Milan: Casa Ricordi, 2000.

Dutilleux, Henri. *Les Citations* for oboe, harpsichord, double bass, and percussion. Paris: Alphonse Leduc, 1985–1990.

Eder, Helmut. *Concerto, Op. 35* for oboe and orchestra. Kassel, Germany: Bärenreiter, 1963.

Eisma, Will. *Diaphonia* for oboe and string trio. Amsterdam: Donemus, 1962.

———. *Fleur minoir* for reed trio. Amsterdam: Donemus, 1984.

———. *Little Lane* for oboe and orchestra. Amsterdam: Donemus, 1973.

Feldman, Morton. *Instruments III* for flute, oboe, and percussion. London: Universal Edition, 1977.

———. *Oboe and Orchestra*. London: Universal Edition, 1976.

Ferneyhough, Brian. *Allgebrah*, for oboe solo and strings. London: Edition Peters, 1996.

———. *Perspectivae Corporum Irregulorum* for oboe, viola, and piano. London: Edition Peters, 1975.

Fine, Vivian. *Music* for flute, oboe, cello. Newton Center, Mass.: Margun, 1980.

———. *Quintet* for oboe, clarinet, violin, cello, and piano. Newton Center, Mass.: Margun, 1984.

———. *Quintet: After Paintings by Edvard Munch* for oboe, clarinet, violin, violoncello, and piano. New York: Henmar Press, Inc., 1985; distributed by Edition Peters.

Finnissy, Michael. *Dilok* for oboe and percussion. London: United Music Publishers Ltd., 1982.

Foss, Lukas. *Concerto* for oboe and orchestra. New York: Peermusic Classical, 1948.

———. *Wind Quintet: The Cave of the Winds*. Paris: Éditions Salabert, 1972.

Francaix, Jean. *L'horage de Flore* for oboe and orchestra. Bryn Mawr, Pa.: Theodore Presser Co., 1959.

Freedman, Harry. *Quintette à vent*. Toronto: E.C. Kirby, 1972.

Fulkerson, James. *Woodwind Quintet 1 & 2*. Karlsruhe, Germany: Edition Modern, 1965, 1966.

Funk, Eric. *Concerto for Oboe, Op. 57*. Manuscript, 1992.

Garcia, Orlando. *Una luz en la neblina distante* for oboe and strings. Manuscript, 1993.

———. *Una luz en la neblina distante* for oboe and four percussion. Manuscript, 2000.

Globokar, Vinko. *Ausstrahlungen* for oboe ad lib and 20 instruments. Peters, 1971.

———. *Convergent—Divergent* for oboe, flute and clarinet. Paris: Editions Ricordi.

———. *Discours VIII* for woodwind quintet. Paris: Editions Ricordi, 1990.

———. *Laboratorium* for 12 musicians. Peters, 1973.

———. *Vendre le Vent* for piano, percussion, and 8 winds. New York: C.F. Peters Corp., 1972.

Goosens, Eugène. *Concerto en un Mouvement*. Paris: Alphonse Leduc, 1960.

Gorecki, Henryk. *Quartettino, Op. 5* for two flutes, oboe, and violin. Kraków, Poland: PWM Edition, 1956.

Gryc, Stephen. *Fantasy Variations on a Theme of Béla Bartók* for oboe and string orchestra. Manuscript, 1992.

Gubaidulina, Sophia. *Concordanze* for woodwind quintet, percussion, violin, viola, cello, and bass. Hamburg: Hans Sikorski, 1971.

Harbison, John. *Oboe Concerto*. New York: G. Schirmer, Inc., 1992.

———. *Quintet for Winds*. New York: G. Schirmer, Inc., 1979.

————. *Snow Country* for oboe and string quintet. New York: G. Schirmer, Inc., 1979.

Harrison, Lou. *Siciliana* for woodwind quintet. New Music Editions, Peters, 1945.

————. *Solstice* for oboe and mixed ensemble. New Music Editions, Peters, 1945.

Harvey, Jonathan. *Death of Light; Light of Death* for oboe, harp, violin, viola, cello. London: Faber Music, 1998.

Hatzis, Christos. *Of Threads and Labyrinths* for oboe, harp, and tape. Manuscript, 1994.

Henze, Hans Werner. *Autunno* for woodwind quintet. Mainz, Germany: Schott Musik International, 1977.

————. *Canzona per sette strumenti*. Mainz, Germany: Schott Musik International, 1982.

————. *Double Concerto* for oboe, harp, and strings. Mainz, Germany: Schott Musik International, 1966.

————. *Quintetto* for woodwind quintet. Mainz, Germany: Schott Musik International, 1952.

Hiller, Lejaran. *Persiflage* for flute, oboe, and percussion. Waterloo, Ontario: Waterloo Music Co., 1977.

Holliger, Heinz. *"h": für Bläserquintett*. Mainz, Germany: Ars Viva Verlag, 1968.

————. *Mobile* for oboe and harp. Mainz, Germany: Schott Musik International, 1962.

————. *Quintetto* for piano and winds. Mainz, Germany: Schott Musik International, 1982.

————. *Schwarzgewobene Trauer: Studie für Sopran, Oboe, Violoncello und Cembalo* Mainz, Germany: Ars Viva Verlag, 1961/62.

————. *Sechs Stücke* for oboe (also oboe d'amore) and harp. Mainz, Germany: Schott Musik International, 1995–99.

————. *Siebengesang: für Oboe, Orchester, Singstimmen und Lautsprecher*. Mainz, Germany: Schott Musik International, 1967.

————. *Spiele* for oboe and harp. Mainz, Germany: Ars Viva Verlag, 1966.

————. *Trio* for oboe, viola, and harp. Mainz, Germany: Ars Viva Verlag/Schott Musik International, 1966.

Hovda, Eleanor. *Beginnings* for oboe/shenai and electric bass. Manuscript, 1991.

————. *Borealis Music* for flute, oboe, bassoon, and piano. Manuscript, 1987.

————. *Record of an Ocean Cliff* for oboe and electric guitar. Manuscript, 1994.

Hovhaness, Alan. *Divertimento* for oboe, clarinet, horn, bassoon. New York: C.F. Peters Corp., 1958.

————. *Prelude and fugue, Op. 13* for oboe and bassoon. New York: C.F. Peters Corp., 1967.

————. *Sonata* for oboe and bassoon, Op. 302. New York: Peer International Corp., 1979.

————. *Sonata, Op. 302* for oboe and bassoon. New York: Peer International Corp., 1977.

————. *Suite* for oboe and bassoon, Op. 23. New York: C.F. Peters Corp., 1968.

————. *Wind Quintet, Op. 159*. New York: C.F. Peters Corp., 1965.

Jaffe, David A. *Number Man* for oboe with SATB soloists and optional chorus. Manuscript, 1990.

Jaffe, Stephen. *Chamber Concerto "Singing Figures"* for oboe and five instruments. Bryn Mawr, Pa.: Merion Music, 1994; distributed by Theodore Presser Co., 1994.

Janacek, Leos. *Mladi* (Youth) for mixed winds. New York City: International Music, 1924.

Jarvinen, Arthur. *Philifor Honeycombed with Childishness* oboe concerto. Los Angeles: Leisure Planet Music, 1991.

Johnson, Tom. *Movements* for woodwind quintet. Paris: Editions 75, 1980.

Johnston, Benjamin. *A Sea Dirge* for Mezzo soprano, flute, oboe, and violin. Urbana, Ill.: Smith Publications, 1962.

————. *Five Fragments* for alto, oboe, bassoon, and cello. Urbana, Ill.: Smith Publications, 1960.

Jolas, Betsy. *O Wall* for woodwind quintet. Paris: Heugel et cie., 1976.

Jolivet, André. *Controversia* for oboe and harp. Billandot, 1968.

————. *Sonatina* for oboe and bassoon. London: Boosey & Hawkes, 1963.

Jordanova, Victoria. *Mute Dance* for harp, oboe, and tape. New York: Compcomp Press, 1994.

Kasemets, Udo. *Octagonal Octet and/or Ode* for 1, 2, 4, 6 or 8 players. Don Mills, Ontario: BMI Canada, 1967.

————. *Trigon* for 1, 3 9, or 27 players. Don Mills, Ontario: BMI Canada, 1963.

Knussen, Oliver. *Cantata, Op. 15* for oboe, violin, viola, and cello. London: Faber Music, 1977.

————. *Processionals, Op. 2* for woodwind quintet. London: Faber Music, 1978.

————. *Three Little Fantasies Op. 6a* for woodwind quintet. London: Faber Music, 1970.

Kotonski, Wlodzimierz. *Concerto per Oboe e Orchestra.* Celle, Germany: Editions Moeck, 1972.

Krenek, Ernst. *Alpbach Quintet, Op. 180* for woodwind quintet and percussion. Vienna: Universal Edition, 1962.

————. *Kitharaulos* for oboe, harp, and chamber orchestra. Vienna: Doblinger, 1971.

————. *Pentagram* for woodwind quintet. Kassel, Germany: Bärenreiter, 1958.

————. *They Knew What They Wanted* for oboe, narrator, piano, percussion, and tape. New York: Rongwen Music, 1977.

Kupferman, Meyer. *Cabaletta* for flute, oboe, and clarinet. Rhinebeck, N.Y.: Soundspells Productions, 1989.

————. *Digitorium* for flute, oboe, and clarinet. Rhinebeck, N.Y.: Soundspells Productions, 1989.

Laderman, Ezra. *A Single Voice* for oboe and strings. New York: Oxford University Press, 1967.

————. *Woodwind sketches.* New York: American Composers Alliance, 1957.

Lang, David. *Frag* for flute, oboe, and cello. New York: Red Poppy Music, 1985; distributed by G. Schirmer, Inc.

Larson, Libby. *Impromptu* for reed trio. New York: G. Schirmer, Inc., 1979.

Lavista, Mario. *Cinco Danzas Breves* for woodwind quintet. México D.F.: Ediciones Mexicanas de Música, 1994.

————. *Marsias* for oboe and at least 8 crystal cups. México, D.F.: Ediciones Mexicanas de Música, 1985.

Lazarof, Henri. *Concerto for Oboe and Chamber Orchestra.* Bryn Mawr, Pa.: Merion Music, 1996; distributed by Theodore Presser Co.

————. *Quintet for Oboe and String Quartet.* Bryn Mawr, Pa.: Merion Music, 1998: distributed by Theodore Presser Co.

————. *Trio* for flute, oboe, and clarinet. Bryn Mawr, Pa.: Merion Music, 1982; distributed by Theodore Presser Co.

Leach, Mary Jane. *Windjammer* for oboe, clarinet, and bassoon. New York: Ariadne Music, 1995.

LeFanu, Nicola. *Variations* for oboe and string trio. London: Chester Music and Novello & Co., 1968.

Lehmann, Hans Ulrich. *Dis-Cantus I* for oboe and string orchestra. Mainz, Germany: Ars Viva Verlag, 1971.

————. *Spiele* for oboe and harp. Mainz, Germany: Ars Viva Verlag, 1966.

————. *Tractus* for flute, oboe, and clarinet. Mainz, Germany: Ars Viva Verlag, 1971.

Ligeti, György. *Double Concerto* for oboe, flute and orchestra. Mainz, Germany: Schott Musik International, 1972.

————. *Six Bagatelles* for woodwind quintet. Mainz, Germany: Schott Musik International, 1953.

————. *Ten Pieces* for woodwind quintet. Mainz, Germany: Schott Musik International, 1968.

Lucier, Alvin. *Concertino* for oboe and string orchestra. Manuscript, 1953.

————. *Serenade for Oboe and Strings* for oboe and string quartet. Frankfurt: Material Press, 1993.

Luening, Otto. *Dealer's Choice: A Divertimento for Oboe, Clarinet & Bassoon.* Rhinebeck, N.Y.: Phantom Press, 1991.

————. *Legend* for oboe and string orchestra. Boston: E.C. Schirmer, Boston, 1951.

————. *The Bass with the Delicate Air: Ostinato for Flute, Oboe, Clarinet & Bassoon.* New York: Composers Facsimile Edition, 1958.

Lutoslawski, Witold. *Double Concerto* for oboe, harp, and chamber orchestra. London: Chester Music and Novello & Co., 1980.

————. *Trio* for oboe, clarinet and bassoon. Manuscript, 1945.

Maderna, Bruno. *Concerto Nr. 3* for three oboes and orchestra. Paris: Éditions Salabert, 1973.

————. *Konzert Nr. 1* for oboe and chamber ensemble. Milan: Edizioni Suvini Zerboni, 1963.

Mamlok, Ursula. *Concerto for Oboe and Orchestra.* Manuscript, 1976.

————. *Festive Sounds* for woodwind quintet. New York: C.F. Peters Corp., 1978.

Martin, Frank. *Three Dances* for oboe, harp, and string orchestra. Vienna: Universal Edition, 1970.

Martino, Donald. *Cinque Frammenti* for oboe and bass. New York: McGinnis & Marx, 1964.

Maxwell Davies, Peter. *Strathclyde Concerto No. 1* for oboe and orchestra. London: Boosey & Hawkes, 1988.

Morricone, Ennio. *Sextet* for flute, oboe, bassoon, violin, viola, and cello, 1955.

Moss, Lawrence. *Unseen Leaves*: a theatrepiece for soprano, oboe, tapes, and lights. Manuscript, 1975.

Musgrave, Thea. *Helios: Concerto for Oboe and Orchestra*. London: Chester Music and Novello & Co., 1994.

———. *Impromptu No. 1* for flute and oboe. London: Chester Music and Novello & Co., 1967.

———. *Impromptu No. 2* for clarinet and oboe. London: Chester Music and Novello & Co., 1970.

Newman, Maria. *Quartet for oboe and string trio*. Manuscript.

Norgard, Per. *Virvelvindens verden (Mondo turbinsoso)* for woodwind quintet. Copenhagen: W. Hansen, 1970.

Oliveros, Pauline. *The Witness* for solo duet with an imaginary partner, a duo or an ensemble. Kingstown, N.Y.: Deep Listening Publications, 1989.

Pärt, Arvo. *Collage über B-A-C-H* for oboe, harpsichord, piano, and strings. Vienna: Universal Edition, 1964.

———. *Fratres* for oboe, clarinet, horn, bassoon, strings, and percussion. Vienna: Universal Edition, 1977.

Partch, Harry. *Bless This House* for oboe, voice, viola, castor, kithara, and mazda marimba. Manuscript, 1961.

———. *Bless This House*. Edited by Adam Silverman. Manuscript, 1961, ed. 1996.

Penderecki, Krysztof. *Capriccio for Oboe and 11 Strings*. Celle, Germany: Editions Moeck, 1965.

Perry, Jeffrey. *The Thrush*. Baton Rouge, La.: What's That Noise Music, 1982.

Porter, Quincy. *Quintet for Oboe and Strings*. Boston: E.C. Schirmer, 1966.

Previn, André. *Trio* for piano, oboe, and bassoon. London: Chester Music and Novello & Co., 1996.

Rands, Bernard. *Concertino* for oboe and ensemble. Miami, Fla.: Helicon Music Corp., 1998.

Reynolds, Roger. *Gathering* for woodwind quintet. New York: C.F. Peters Corp., 1965.

———. *On the Balance of Things* for oboe, chamber ensemble, and tape. New York: C.F. Peters Corp., 1996.

Richards, Stephen. *Prayer: Suite for Oboe and Strings*. California: Stephen Richards Music Publications, 1994.

Rihm, Wolfgang. *Musik für Oboe und Orchester*. Vienna: Universal Editions, 1997.

Rochberg, George. *Concerto for Oboe and Orchestra*. Bryn Mawr, Pa.: Theodore Presser Co., 1983.

———. *Duo* for oboe and bassoon. Bryn Mawr, Pa.: Theodore Presser Co., 1976.

Rorem, Ned. *After Long Silence* for voice, oboe, and strings. London: Boosey & Hawkes, 1982.

———. *Lovers* for harpsichord, oboe, cello, and percussion. London: Boosey & Hawkes, 1964.

Roseman, Ronald. *Come Chitarra for Oboe and Guitar*. Richmond, Va.: International Opus, 1988.

———. *Psalm 42 for Chorus, Oboe and String Orchestra*. New York: American Composers Alliance, 1993.

———. *Sonata a Tre* for flute, oboe, and cello. New York: American Composers Alliance, 1995.

———. *Trio for Oboe, Trombone and Piano*. New York: American Composers Alliance, 1985.

Rosenboom, David. *In the Beginning II* for woodwind quintet. Santa Clarita, Calif.: David Rosenboom Publishing, 1979.

Roxburgh, Edwin. *Constellations* for descant recorder and oboe. London: United Music Publishers Ltd., 1973.

———. *Ecclissi* for oboe and string trio. London: United Music Publishers Ltd., 1971.

Rypdal, Terje. *Shadow, Op. 16* for oboe, four trombones, percussion, and strings. Manuscript, 1980.

Saariaho, Kaija. *Sah den Vogeln* for soprano, flute, oboe, cello, piano, and electronics. Copenhagen: W. Hansen, 1981.

Salonen, Esa-Pekka. *Mimo II* for solo oboe and chamber ensemble. New York: G. Schirmer, Inc., 1992.

———. *Prologue* for oboe, violin, cello, and percussion. Hameerlinna, Finland: Jasemusiikki, 1980.

Sanchez, Carlos. *M. E. in Memoriam* for oboe solo with small miscellaneous chamber ensemble. Manuscript, 1995.

Scelsi, Giacinto. *IXOR* for oboe and ensemble. Paris: Éditions Salabert, 1984.

———. *Rucke di Guck* for piccolo and oboe. Paris: Éditions Salabert, 1957.

Schat, Peter. *Improvisations and Symphonies* for wind quintet. Amsterdam: Donemus, 1960.

Schickele, Peter. *Commedia* for two oboes and bassoon. Bryn Mawr, Pa.: Elkan-Vogel, Inc., 1979.

Schnittke, Alfred. *Double Concerto* for oboe, harp, and strings. Vienna: Universal Edition, 1971.

———. *Moz-art* for oboe, harp, harpsichord, violin, violoncello, and double bass. Hamburg: Hans Sikorski, 1995.

Schuller, Gunther. *Trio* for oboe, horn, and viola. New York: Associated Music Publishers, Inc., 1975.

———. *Woodwind quintet*. London: Schott & Co. Ltd., 1958.

Schuman, William. *Dances* for wind quintet and percussion. Bryn Mawr, Pa.: Merion Music, 1987; distributed by Theodore Presser Co.

———. *To Thee Old Cause* for oboe, brass, timpani, piano, and strings. Bryn Mawr, Pa.: Merion Music, 1971; distributed by Theodore Presser Co.

Schwartz, Elliott. *Aria No. 5*. New York: Carl Fischer, 1968.

———. *By George* for oboe, cello, and piano. New York: American Composers Alliance, 2004.

———. *Music for Audience and Soloist*. New York: American Composers Alliance, 1970.

———. *Quartet* for oboe and strings. St. Louis, Mo.: Norruth Music, 1963.

Shapey, Ralph. *Oboe Quartet* for oboe and strings. Bryn Mawr, Pa.: Theodore Presser Co, 1952.

———. *Psalm I* for oboe, soprano, and piano. Bryn Mawr, Pa.: Theodore Presser Co., 1984.

Sims, Ezra. *From an Oboe Quartet*. New York: American Composers Edition, 1971.

Singer, Lawrence. *Concerto per Lothar* for oboe solo, strings, and percussion. Milan: Edizioni Suvini Zerboni, 1991.

———. *Grandmother's Attic* for flute, oboe, violin, cello. Blaine, Minn.: Jeanné, Inc., 1980.

———. *Musica a due: per oboe e chitarra*. Milan: Edizioni Suvini Zerboni, 1965.

———. *Sensazione II for Solo Oboe with Diverse Instruments*. Manuscript, 1983.

Smit, Leo. *In Woods* for oboe, harp, and percussion. New York: Carl Fischer, 1978.

———. *Suite* for oboe and cello. Amsterdam: Donemus, 1938.

Smith, Stuart. *Faces* for oboe and clarinet. Baltimore: Smith Publications, 1978.

Sollberger, Harvey. *Three or Four Things I Know about the Oboe*. New York: McGinnis & Marx, 1986.

Steinke, Greg. *Music for Chief Joseph* for oboe and four trombones. Newton, Mass.: Frank E. Warren Music Service, 1980, rev. 1995.

Stockhausen, Karlheinz. *Tierkreis*. Kürten, Germany: Stockhausen-Verlag, 1976.

———. *Zeitmasze* for woodwind quintet. Kürten, Germany: Stockhausen-Verlag: 1956.

Takahashi, Yuji. *Operation Euler* for 2 or 3 oboes. New York: C.F. Peters Corp., 1969.

Takemitsu, Toru. *Entre-temps* for oboe and string quartet. Mainz, Germany: Schott Musik International, 1987.

———. *Eucalyptus II* for flute, oboe, and harp. Paris: Éditions Salabert, 1971.

———. *Gemeaux I* for oboe and trombone with orchestra. Paris: Éditions Salabert, 1974.

Tenney, James. *Critical Band* for variable ensemble and tape delay. Lebanon, N.H.: Frog Peak Music, 1988.

———. *Spectrum 2* for woodwind quintet. Lebanon, N.H.: Frog Peak Music, 1995.

———. *Thirteen Ways of Looking at a Blackbird* for bass voice, alto flute-flute, oboe, viola, cello, bass. Baltimore: Sonic Art Editions/Smith Publications, 1971.

Tower, Joan. *Island Prelude* for oboe and string quintet. New York: G. Schirmer, Inc., 1989.

Tréfousse, Roger. *Jackson Pollock Suite* (Version for Eight Instruments). New York: American Composers Alliance.

Weir, Judith. *Mountain Airs* for flute, clarinet, and oboe. London: Chester Music and Novello & Co.: 1988.

Wernick, Richard. *Oracle II* for oboe, soprano, and piano. Bryn Mawr, Pa.: Theodore Presser Co., 1985.

Wildberger, Jacques. *Concerto* for oboe and orchestra. Cologne, Germany: Edition Gerig, 1963.

———. *Quartet* for flute, oboe, harp, and piano. Cologne, Germany: Edition Gerig, 1967.

———. *Trio* for reed trio. Cologne, Germany: Edition Gerig, 1952.

Wilder, Alec. *Piece for Oboe and Improvisatory Percussion*. Newton Center, Mass.: Margun Music, 1959.

———. *Suite* for harp, oboe, and French horn. Newton Center, Mass.: Margun Music, 1979.

———. *Suite* for oboe, clarinet, and bassoon. Newton Center, Mass.: Margun Music, 1969.

Wilson, Richard. *Deux Pas de Trois* for flute, oboe, and harpsichord. New York: Peermusic Classical, 1979.

———. *Dithyramb* for oboe and clarinet. New York: Southern Music Publishing, 1983; distributed by Peermusic Classical.

———. *Gnomics* for flute, oboe, and clarinet. New York: Southern Music Publishing, 1981; distributed by Peermusic Classical.

Wolpe, Stefan. *Quartett* for oboe, cello, piano, and percussion. New York: McGinnis & Marx, 1958.

———. *Suite Im Hexachord* for oboe and clarinet. New York: McGinnis & Marx, 1936.

Xenakis, Iannis. *Dmaathen* for oboe and percussion. Paris: Éditions Salabert, 1976.

Yun, Isang. *Images* for oboe, flute, violin, and cello. Berlin: Bote & Bock, 1968.

———. *Konzert* for oboe and orchestra. Berlin: Bote & Bock, 1990.

———. *Rondell* for reed trio. Berlin: Bote & Bock, 1975.

———. *Rufe* for oboe and harp. Berlin: Bote & Bock, 1989.

———. *Trio* for oboe, flute, and violin. Berlin: Bote & Bock, 1973.

Zaimont, Judith. *3:4,5* for oboe, clarinet, violin, viola, and bass. Blaine, Minn.: Jeanné, Inc., 1997.

———. *Dance/Inner Dance* for oboe, flute, and cello. Amityville, N.Y.: Sounds Alive!, 1985.

Zimmermann, Bernd Alois. *Concerto* for oboe and orchestra. Mainz, Germany: Schott Musik International, 1952.

Zonn, Paul. *After-Images* for double-reed quintet. Manuscript, 1978.

———. *Canzonni, Overo Sonate Concertare Conserere* for oboe and eight players. New York: American Composers Alliance, 1974.

———. *Microditties* for oboe and string trio. New York: American Composers Alliance, 1967.

Zwilich, Ellen Taaffe. *Concerto* for oboe and orchestra. Bryn Mawr, Pa.: Merion Music, 1990; distributed by Theodore Presser Co.

English Horn with Miscellaneous Larger Ensembles

Badings, Henk. *Concerto*. Amsterdam: Donemus, 1975.

Bartolozzi, Bruno. *The Solitary* for English horn and percussion. Milan: Edizioni Suvini Zerboni, 1976.

Bernstein, Charles Harold. *Dimensions* for English horn and percussion. Culver City, Calif.: Siempre Musica, 1996.

Copland, Aaron. *Quiet City* for English horn, trumpet, and strings. London: Boosey & Hawkes, 1942.

Honegger, Arthur. *Concerto di camera* for flute, English horn, and strings. Copenhagen: W. Hansen, 1948.

Hovda, Eleanor. *Crossings in a Mountain Dream* for English horn and electric bass. Manuscript, 1995.

Jolas, Betsy. *Remember* for English horn and cello. Paris: Heugel et cie., 1971.

Kernis, Aaron. *Colored Field* for English horn and orchestra. New York: Associated Music Publishers, Inc., 1994.

Knussen, Oliver. *Alleluya Nativitatis* for woodwind quintet (with English horn rather than oboe). London: Faber Music, 1987.

———. *Elegiac Arabesques Op. 26a* for English horn and clarinet. London: Faber Music, 1991.

Macbride, David. *Rozmarin* for English horn quartet and offstage oboe. Manuscript, 1996.

MacMillan, James. *The World's Ransoming* for English horn and orchestra. London: Boosey & Hawkes, 1997.

Persichetti, Vincent. *English Horn Concerto*. Bryn Mawr, Pa.: Theodore Presser Co., 1977.

Powell, Mel. *Cantilena Concertante* for English horn and orchestra. New York: G. Schirmer, Inc., 1948.

Rorem, Ned. *Concerto for English Horn*. London: Boosey & Hawkes, 1997.

Roseman, Ronald. *Concertino for English Horn and Strings*. New York: American Composers Alliance, 1983.

Silverman, Faye-Ellen. *Echoes of Emily* for alto and English horn. New York: Seesaw Music Corp., 1979.

Skrowaczewski, Stanislow. *Concerto* for English horn and orchestra. New York: G. Schirmer, Inc., 1970.

Tréfousse, Roger. *Column*. Manuscript, 1980.

Oboe d'Amore and Bass Oboe Pieces

Bell, Derek. *Nocturne on an Icelandic Melody* for oboe d'amore (opt. oboe) and harp. West Linn, Oreg.: Amoris International, 1983.

Blezard, William. *Two Contrasted Pieces* for oboe d'amore (opt. oboe) and piano. West Linn, Oreg.: Amoris International, 1994.

Bryars, Gavin. *The East Coast* for bass oboe and chamber orchestra. Manuscript, 1994.

Carr, Edwin. *Four Pieces* for oboe d'amore (opt. English horn) and piano. West Linn, Oreg.: Amoris International, 1967.

———. *Prelude and Aria* for oboe d'amore (opt. English horn) and piano. West Linn, Oreg.: Amoris International, 1990.

———. *Two Mansfield Poems* for oboe d'amore (opt. English horn) and piano. West Linn, Oreg.: Amoris International, 1988.

Deak, Jon. *Oboe d'Amore Concerto*. Manuscript, 1996.

Epstein, Marti. *Thalia* for oboe d'amore and live electronics. Manuscript.

Holliger, Heinz. *Vier Miniaturen* for oboe d'amore, soprano, celeste, and harp. Mainz, Germany: Schott Musik International, 1963.

Hovda, Eleanor. *Glacier Track* for oboe d'amore and electric bass. Manuscript, 1996.

Maderna, Bruno. *Aulodia per Lothar* for oboe d'amore (and guitar, ad. lib). Milan: Edizioni Suvini Zerboni, 1965.

———. *Solo* for oboe (or musette, oboe d'amore, or English horn). Milan: Casa Ricordi, 1971.

Marshall, Ingram. *Holy Ghosts* for oboe d'amore and digital delay units. Hamden, Conn.: IBU Music, 2000.

Martin, Frank. *Sonata da chiesa* for oboe d'amore and organ. Vienna: Universal Edition, 1938.

Marx, Karl. *Sechs Miniaturen* for oboe d'amore and harpsichord. Kassel, Germany: Bärenreiter, 1974.

Morricone, Ennio. *Twelve Variations* for oboe d'amore, cello, and piano. 1956.

Takemitsu, Toru. *Vers, l'arc-en-ciel, Palma* for guitar, oboe d'amore, and orchestra. Tokyo: Schott Japan, 1989.

Vees, Jack. *Gloria* for oboe d'amore and Hammond organ. Los Angeles: Leisure Planet Music, 2000.

Etudes

Bozza, Eugène. *Graphismes* (Graphic Notations for the reading of different contemporary musical graphic notations for solo oboe). Paris: Alphonse Leduc, 1975.

Castanié, Gérard. *Et in Arcadia Ego* (22 pieces for solo oboe). Paris: Alphonse Leduc, 1990.

Jarvinen, Arthur. *Experimental Etudes*. Los Angeles: Leisure Planet Music, 1996.

Luttmann, Reinhard. *Vingt et Une Etudes Dodécaphoniques* (Twenty-One Dodecaphonic Studies). Paris: Alphonse Leduc, 1969.

~

Selected Literature Bibliography

Books

Backus, William. *The Acoustical Foundations of Music*. New York: W.W. Norton & Company, 1977.

Bartolozzi, Bruno. *New Sounds for Woodwind*. Translated and edited by Reginald Smith Brindle. London: Oxford University Press, 1967, rev. 1982.

Bate, Philip. *The Oboe: An Outline of its History, Development, and Construction*, 3rd ed. London: Ernest Benn Ltd., 1975.

Benade, Arthur. *Fundamentals of Musical Acoustics*. London: Oxford University Press, 1976.

———. *Horns, Strings, and Harmony*. New York: Doubleday and Co., 1960.

Burgess, Geoffrey, and Bruce Haynes. *The Oboe*. New Haven: Yale University Press, 2004.

Chenna, Andrea, with Massimiliano Salmi and Omar Zoboli. *Manuale Dell'Oboe Contemporaneo* [The Contemporary Oboe]. Milan: Rugginenti Editore, Milan, 1994.

Davis, Gary, and Mark Jones. *Sound Reinforcement Handbook*. Milwaukee, Wisc.: Hal Leonard Publishing Co., 1987.

Dick, Robert. *The Other Flute: A Performance Manual of Contemporary Techniques*, 2nd ed. New York: Multiple Breath Music Company, 1989.

Dobson, Richard. *A Dictionary of Electronic and Computer Music Technology*. Oxford: Oxford University Press, 1992.

Glaetzner, Burkhard. *Spielmöglichkeiten und Notationsvorschläge*. Leipzig, Germany: Edition Peters, 1978.

Goldstein, Malcolm. *Sounding the Full Circle*. Manuscript, 1988. Available at www.mcgill.ca/improv/mgoldstein/sounding/.

Goosens, Leon, and Edwin Roxburgh. *Oboe*. Yehudi Menuhin Music Guides. London: Macdonald and Jane's, 1977.

Holliger, Heinz, ed. *Pro Musica Nova, Studies for Playing Avant-garde Music for the Oboe*. Wiesbaden, Germany: Breitkopf & Hartel, 1972.

Ledet, David. *Oboe Reed Styles*. Bloomington: Indiana University Press, 1981.

Light, Jay. *The Oboe Reed Book*. Des Moines, Iowa: Drake University, 1983.

Nederveen, Cornelius. *Acoustical Aspects of Wind Instruments*. Amsterdam: Frits Knuf, 1969.

Read, Gardner. *Contemporary Instrumental Techniques*. New York: Schirmer Books, 1976.

Rehfeldt, Phillip. *New Directions for Clarinet*, rev. ed. Berkeley: University of California Press, 1994.

Rothwell, Evelyn. *Oboe Technique*. London: Oxford University Press, 1962.

Singer, Lawrence, and Bruno Bartolozzi. *Metodo per Oboe*. Milan: Edizioni Suvini Zerboni, 1969.

Tomlyn, Bo, and Steve Leonard. *Electronic Music Dictionary*. Milwaukee, Wisc.: Hal Leonard Books, 1988.

Veale, Peter, and Claus-Steffen Mahnkopf. *The Techniques of Oboe Playing*. Kassel, Germany: Bärenreiter, 1994.

Weisberg, Arthur. *The Art of Wind Playing*. New York: Schirmer Books, 1975.

Articles

Aikin, Jim. "'Vocoder Wars'—How Does a Vocoder Work?" *Keyboard* (August 2000): 44.

Benade, Arthur. "On the Mathematical Theory of Woodwind Finger Holes." *Journal of the Acoustical Society of America* 32 (1960): 1591–1608.

———. "On Woodwind Instrument Bores." *Journal of the Acoustical Society of America* 31 (1959): 137–146.

———. "The Physics of Woodwinds." *Scientific American* 203 (October 1960): 145–154.

Cohen, Aaron. "Oboists and Electronics: Embracing a New Era." *International Double Reed Society Journal* 25 (July 1997): 43–49.

Craxton, Janet. "Contemporary Oboe Technique." *The Composers Guild of Great Britain* 43 (Spring 1972): 11–12.

———. "Contemporary Oboe Technique." *To the World's Oboists* 1, no. 1 (Winter 1972–1973): 3–5.

Fonville, John. "Ben Johnston's Extended Just Intonation: A Guide for Interpreters." *Perspectives of New Music* 29, no. 2: 106–135.

Post, Nora. "Monophonic Sound Resources for the Oboe." *Interface: Journal of New Music Research* 11 (1982): 131–176.

———. "Multiphonics for the Oboe." *Interface: Journal of New Music Research* 10, no. 2 (August 1981): 113–136.

Roxburgh, Edwin. "Contemporary Oboe Technique." *The Composers Guild of Great Britain* 76–77 (Summer–Winter 1982): 13–16.

Silverman, Adam. *Notational Styles for Microtonal Just Intonation*. Author's manuscript.

Singer, Lawrence, and Bruno Bartolozzi. "Some Monophonic and Multiphonic Possibilities of the Oboe." *National Association of College Wind and Percussion Instructors Journal* 23 (Spring 1975): 3–10.

———. "Woodwind Development; A Monophonic and Multiphonic Point of View." *Woodwind World* 14 (June 1975): 14.

Steinke, Greg. "New Music and the Oboist." *To the World's Oboists* 4, no. 1 (1976): 4.

———. "New Music and the Oboist II." *To the World's Oboists* 4, no. 3 (1976): 4.

———. "New Music and the Oboist III." *The Double Reed* 2, no. 31 (1979): 37.

———. "New Music and the Oboist III and 1/2." *The Double Reed* 3, no. 2 (1979): 30.

Sullivan, Matthew. "Microtonal Oboe." *Pitch for the International Microtonalist* 1, no. 4 (1990): 80–83.

Van Cleve, Libby. "Suggestions for the Performance of Berio's *Sequenza VII*." *The Double Reed* 13, no. 3 (Winter 1991): 45–51.

Zonn, Wilma. "Observations for Today's Oboist." *The Double Reed* (March 1978): 6–13.

~

Selected Discography

The following compilation is by no means complete. Instead, it is a sampling of CDs that offer non-Western double reeds, jazz oboe, and contemporary classical compositions.

Andriessen, Louis. *Anachrony 2 for Oboe and Orchestra*. Hans de Vries, oboe. Donemus CV54.

Appledorn, Mary Jeanne van. *Incantations*. Amy Anderson, oboe. On *Winds and Voices*, vol. 5. Living Artist Recordings LAR 5.

Arter, Matthias, oboe. *Oboe Plus*. Includes works by W. Feldman, Arter, Berio, N. Huber, and R. Boesch. Col Legno WWE 1CD 20009.

———. *Oboe Solo*. Includes music by Dinescu, Holliger, Lehmann, Marti, and Nicherson, and improvisations. Pan Classics 510-087.

Berio, Luciano. *Sequenza VII*. Heinz Holliger, oboe. Philips 426-662-2.

Bernstein, Charles Harold. *Dimensions*. Kim Gilad, English horn. Arcobaleno (Empire Master Sound Recordings) AAOC-93922.

Bolle, James. *Oboe Concerto*. Basil Reeve, oboe. On *Music of James Bolle*. Gasparo GSCD-317.

Caplan, Stephen, oboe. *A Tree in Your Ear*. Includes works by Bimstein, Still, Hovhannes, Baley, Lateer, and Philips. Musicians Showcase Recordings CD MS70799.

CCM4. *CCM4 Destroys New York*. Rafael Cohen, oboe. Newsonic Label, Newsonic 14. (This is a live recording from this youthful trio of improvisers, Tri-Centric Festival, New York, 1999.)

Celli, Joseph, oboe. *Organic Oboe*. Music by Celli, Stockhausen, Schwartz, and Goldstein. OODiscs OO1.

———. *No World Improvisations* with Jin Hi Kim. OODiscs OO2. (Includes Celli performing on Indian double-reed mukha veena, and Yamaha WX-7.)

———. *No World (Trio) Improvisations* with Jin Hi Kim, Alvin Curran, Shelley Hirsch, Malcolm Goldstein, Mor Thiam, and Adam Plack. OODiscs OO4. (Includes Celli performing on Korean double-reed p'iri, reeds alone, and English horn without reeds.)

Cherney, Lawrence, oboe. *Tongues of Angels*. Music by Keane, Barroso, Tittle, Hatch, Piché, and Traux. Centrediscs WRC8-6696.

Corigliano, John. *Concerto for Oboe and Orchestra*. Bert Lucarelli, oboe. RCA Red Seal ARL 1-2534.

———. *Oboe Concerto*. Winnipeg Symphony Orchestra, Douglas Bairstow, oboe. On *Collage*. WSO records WSOCD 9401.

Farrell, Joe. *Joe Farrell Quartet*. CBS Records ZK 40694. (Includes some oboe playing by this jazz doubler. The ensemble consists of the jazz legends Chick Corea, Dave Holland, Jack DeJohnette, and John McLaughlin.)

Fifth Species. *Inside the Dance of Rain*. Woodwind quintet music by Wolfe, Mott, Komorous, Bresnick, Prezament, Jarvinen, and Ligeti. Libby Van Cleve, oboe. Artifact Music ART-007.

First Avenue. *Shreds of Evidence.* Matt Sullivan, oboe. OODiscs OO50. (This is just one of the many recordings from this innovative New York electro-acoustic improvisation ensemble.)

Funk, Eric. *Concerto for Oboe, Op. 57.* Martin Schuring, oboe. MMC Recordings 2033.

Glaetzner, Burkhard, oboe. *Neue Musik für Oboe.* Music by Yun, Xenakis, Schenker, Berio, and Lombari. Berlin Classics 0011722BC.

Goode, Daniel. *Fiddle Studies.* Libby Van Cleve, oboe. On *Tunnel-Funnel.* Tzadik TZ 7029.

Goyarrola, Aitor. *Premonitions.* GME, Inc. 1996. (Mostly new age and electronic music with Elena Troncone, oboe.)

Hatzis, Christos. *Byzantium.* Libby Van Cleve, oboe. On *Byzantium.* Centrediscs WRC8-6695.

Holliger, Heinz, oboe. *The Artistry of Heinz Holliger.* Music by Penderecki and Holliger. Denon DC-8006.

———. *Duo für Violine und Violinecello, Stüdie uber Mehrklänge für Oboe Solo,* and original compositions. Heinz Holliger, oboe and composer. ECM 1340.

Hovda, Eleanor. *Ariadne Music.* OODiscs OO46.

———. *Coastal Traces.* Includes numerous chamber works, Libby Van Cleve, oboe, oboe d'amore, and English horn. OODiscs OO29.

Hove, Carolyn, oboe and English horn. Music by Hindemith, Salonen, Marvin, Carter, Stevens, and Persichetti. Crystal Records CD328.

Khan, Bismillah. *Shenai Nawaz.* Odeon LP EASD 1512, EMI Records. (Just one of the many recordings of this phenomenal shenai virtuoso.)

Kim, Jin Hi. *Living Tones.* Joseph Celli, oboe, English horn, and Korean double-reed p'iri. OODiscs OO24.

King, Nancy Ambrose, oboe. *The Winning Program.* Includes *Memories for Solo Oboe* by Lawrence Singer and *Three Piece Suite* by Madeline Dring. Boston Records BR1019CD.

Kirk, Rahsaan Roland. *Does Your House Have Lions.* Rhino Records, Atlantic Jazz Gallery R271406. (Includes English horn playing by this multireed jazz artist. Even more remarkable is the cut in which he plays English horn and tenor sax simultaneously.)

Krenek, Ernst. *They Knew What They Wanted* for oboe, narrator, piano, and percussion (1976–1977). James Ostryniec, oboe. Orion Master Recordings (LP) OR 80380.

Lateef, Yusef. *Live at Pep's.* impulse! GRD-134 (This is just one of the many recordings of jazz multi-instrumentalist Lateef. He improvises on oboe, shenai, and argol on this and other recordings. Also recommended is *The Complete Yusef Lateef,* Atlantic Label.)

Leach, Mary Jane. *Windjammer.* Libby Van Cleve, oboe. On *Ariadne's Lament.* New World Records 80525-2.

———. *Xantippe's Rebuke.* Libby Van Cleve, oboe. On *The Aerial #6.* Aeri 994/6.

Ligeti, György. *Melodian/Double Concerto/Chamber Concerto.* Heinz Holliger, oboe soloist. London 425 6232.

Lockwood, Annea. *Thousand Year Dreaming.* Libby Van Cleve, oboe. What Next Recordings WN0010.

Marshall, Ingram. *Dark Waters.* Libby Van Cleve, English horn, oboe d'amore. New Albion Records NA 112 CD.

Moulanna (Sheik Chinna Moulanna Saheb). *Nadhaswaram.* Haus der Kulturen der Welt/Wergo SM 1507-2 281507-2. (Nadhaswaram music from South India.)

One Alternative. *Changes.* Jill Haley, oboe. J-Bird records JBD 80221-2. (This is just one of several releases from this two-guitar and oboe trio playing original music blending folk, jazz, and popular styles, much influenced by the group Oregon.)

Oregon. *Always, Never, and Forever.* Paul McCandless, oboe. Intuition Records INT 2073 2. (This is just one example of the many recordings featuring the innovative improvisational work of McCandless with the group Oregon. Other recommended records are *Together* on the Vanguard Label and his 1979 recording as leader, *All Mornings Bring,* on the Elektra Label.)

Ostryniec, James, oboe. *James Ostryniec, Oboe.* Includes Lutoslawski, *Epitaph;* Shapey, *Sonata;* Seeger, *Three Songs for alto, oboe, piano & percussion;* Ives, Adagio Sostenuto (with string quartet); and Luening, *Legend* for oboe and strings. CRI LP SD501.

————, oboe. *Krenek, Four Pieces; Wuorinen, Composition for Oboe and Piano; Moss, Unseen Leaves for Oboe Soprano and Tape.* Orion Master Recording LP ORS 78288.

————, oboe. *Music for Oboe.* Includes Rochberg, *La Bocca Della Verita*; Seeger, *Diaphonic Suite No. 1*; Shapey, *Rhapsodie*; Schuler, *Trio*; Julian, *Wave Canon*; and Singer, *Work.* CRI SD LP 423.

Paull, Jennifer, oboe d'amore. *The Oboe D'amore Collection, Volume II.* Music by Blezard, Carr, Schiffman, Salzedo, Rushby-Smith, Josephs, and McCabe. Amoris International AI SC VII.

Pillow, Charles. *Currents.* A Recordings AL 73108, distributed by Challenge Records Services, the Netherlands. (Includes some jazz standards performed on oboe.)

Ra, Sun. *Other Planes of There.* Marshall Allen, oboe. Evidence Label ECD 22037. (Sun Ra and his Solar Arkestra, allegedly from ancient Egypt or outer space, perform free jazz, and Allen doubles imaginatively on the oboe. Another recommended recording is *Cosmic Tones for Mental Therapy*, Evidence Label, ECD 22036.)

Reynolds, Roger. *Summer Island.* Jacqueline LeClaire, oboe. On *The Paris Pieces.* Neuma 450-91.

Samul and Hojok Sinawi, Taepungnyu—The Ideal of Korean Traditional Wind Ensemble. Features hojok and p'iri, both Korean double reeds. JVC CD Ethnic Sounds Series #26. VID-25021.

Sargous, Harry, oboe. *Premiere Oboe Works.* Music by Bolcom, Singer, Cowell, and Bassett. Crystal Records CD326.

Schuman-Post, Brenda, oboe. *Oboe of the World.* Hiwood Productions 0108. BSP6263@aol.com. (Includes oboe music influenced by various world music traditions with some improvisation.)

Simpson, Andrew Earle. *Exhortation II.* Nancy Ambrose King, oboe. On *Exhortations.* Athena Records Athena 106.

Sinawi Music of Korea. Features hojok and p'iri, both Korean double reeds. King Record Company 1992 KICC 5163.

Stacy, Thomas, English horn, oboe, and oboe d'amore. *New York Legends.* Music by Berg, Downey, Fuchs, Ravel, Read, and Yvon. Cala Records CACD 0511.

Sumatra/Batak Music. Indonesian Double Reed Playing. Inedit, Maison des Cultures du Monde W260061, France.

Taylor, Cecil. *Unit Structures.* Ken McIntyre, oboe. Blue Note Label CDP 7 84237 2.

Tenney, James. *Critical Band.* On *On Edge*, by Relache. Mode CD22.

Vees, Jack. *Surf Music Again.* Includes *Tattooed Barbie*, Libby Van Cleve, oboe electrified. CRI 730.

Verdery, Benjamin, guitar. *Some Towns and Cities.* Includes chamber works with Vicki Bodner, oboe. Newport Classic NPD 85519.

————. *Ufonia.* New music ensemble playing mostly written, some improvised music, Vicki Bodner, oboe. Mushkatweek Records 100.

Vogel, Allan, oboe. *Oboe Obsession.* Includes works by Saint-Saëns, Britten, Schumann, W. F. Bach, and Shinohara. Delos Records DE 3235.

Weise, Jan. *Stunt.* Electronic pieces performed and composed by Jan Weise. Oslo Impressario label.

Yugoslavian Folk Music of Macedonia. Yugoslavian double-reed (zurla) playing. Olympic Records LP 6130.

Index

~

About the Author

Libby Van Cleve (BA, Bowdoin College; MFA, California Institute of the Arts; MM, MMA, and DMA, Yale School of Music) is recognized as one of the foremost interpreters of contemporary music for the oboe. She has performed as a soloist throughout North America, and her solo playing is featured on the CRI, Aerial, and Centrediscs CD labels. Her solo English horn and oboe d'amore performances are featured on the recently released CD *Dark Waters*, music by Ingram Marshall. This disc has met with critical acclaim both nationally and internationally.

In addition, Ms. Van Cleve performs regularly with chamber music groups, including Chez Vees and Burning Bush Baroque. Compact discs featuring her chamber playing have been released on the Tzadik, New World, OODisc, Braxton House, What Next?, CRI, and Artifact labels. Numerous compositions have been written for her and have been commissioned by organizations such as the National Endowment for the Arts, Connecticut Commission for the Arts, Canada Council, and Minnesota Composers Forum.

In addition to *Oboe Unbound*, Ms. Van Cleve is coauthor, along with Vivian Perlis, of a forthcoming book/CD publication on oral history perspectives of contemporary American music, to be published by Yale University Press. She also edited Bach's Suites Numbers 1 and 3, available through T. D. Ellis Music Publishing, ASCAP.

Ms. Van Cleve currently resides in New Haven, Connecticut, with her husband, Jack Vees, and daughter, Nola.

Names of Notes

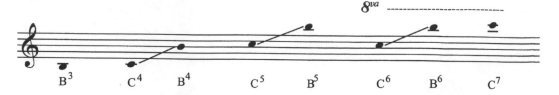

B^3 C^4 B^4 C^5 B^5 C^6 B^6 C^7

Symbols

▽ tip of reed	⬬ strong lip pressure (biting)	■ strong air pressure
▽ just below heart	⊖ medium lip pressure	▣ weak air pressure
▽ at string	◯ weak lip pressure	☐ medium air pressure

Oboe Keys

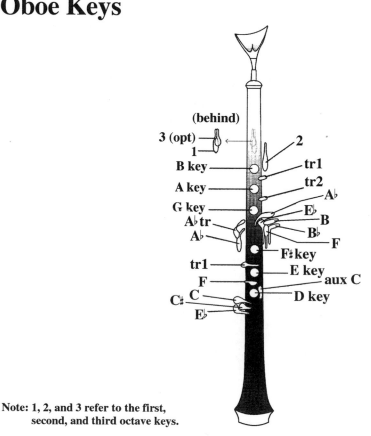

(behind)

3 (opt)
1
B key
A key
G key
A♭ tr
A♭

2
tr1
tr2
A♭
E♭
B
B♭
F

tr1
F
C♯ C
E♭

F♯ key
E key
aux C
D key

Note: 1, 2, and 3 refer to the first,
second, and third octave keys.